HTML5 and CSS3 Responsive Web Design Cookbook

Learn the secrets of developing responsive websites capable of interfacing with today's mobile Internet devices

Benjamin LaGrone

PUBLISHING

BIRMINGHAM - MUMBAI

HTML5 and CSS3 Responsive Web Design Cookbook

First published: May 2013

Production Reference: 1160513

Published by Packt Publishing Ltd.
Livery Place
35 Livery Street
Birmingham B3 2PB, UK.

ISBN 978-1-84969-544-2

www.packtpub.com

Cover Image by Duraid Fatouhi (duraidfatouhi@yahoo.com)

Credits

Author

Benjamin LaGrone

Reviewers

Dale Cruse

Ed Henderson

Rokesh Jankie

Acquisition Editor

Edward Gordon

Lead Technical Editors

Savio Jose

Neeshma Ramakrishnan

Technical Editors

Ishita Malhi

Hardik Soni

Nitee Shetty

Project Coordinator

Arshad Sopariwala

Proofreader

Amy Guest

Indexer

Tejal R. Soni

Production Coordinator

Nitesh Thakur

Cover Work

Nitesh Thakur

About the Author

Benjamin LaGrone is a web developer who lives and works in Texas. He got his start in programming at the age of 6 when he took his first computer class at The Houston Museum of Natural Science. His first program was "choose your own adventure book", written in BASIC; he has fond memories of the days when software needed you to write line numbers.

Fast forward to about thirty years later; after deciding that computers are here to stay, Ben has made a career combining some of his favorite things—art and coding; creating art from code. One of his favorite projects was using the GMaps API to map pathologies to chromosomes for cancer research.

Fascinated with mobile devices for a long time, Ben thinks that the Responsive Web is one of the most exciting, yet long time coming, new aspects of web development. He now works in a SAAS development shop and is the mobile and Responsive Web evangelist for the team.

When he's not working on some Internet project, Ben spends his time building robots, tinkering with machines, drinking coffee, surfing, and teaching Kuk Sool martial arts.

This book could not have been written without the patience and support of my loving wife, Hannah, and my two beautiful daughters, Daphne and Darby. Thank you.

About the Reviewers

Dale Cruse is the author of *HTML5 Multimedia Development* and has worked as a technical editor on several other HTML5 books. He started his career in 1995 as a U.S. Army photojournalist. Since going purely digital on CBSNews.com, he's created web and mobile experiences for some of the most well-known clients in the world, including 20th Century Fox, Bloomingdale's, and MINI Cooper. Currently, he juggles between being a senior frontend developer at Allen & Gerritsen and a New York Yankees fan in South Boston. An in-demand speaker, you can't get him to shut up on Twitter at @dalecruse.

Ed Henderson was born and raised in Scotland, and is an experienced human being, with a love for designing, building, and making and breaking things online.

Not afraid to get his hands dirty and his feet wet, he is open to new technologies as long as they are useful and/or fun.

Ed has a real degree in Computer Science, has run his own business, worked freelance, been employed, and been a consultant. He is now employed as Senior Software Engineer for POPSUGAR in San Francisco, California, USA.

He has vast experience in all aspects of the industry, from web pages and apps to social media. Ed has also reviewed and written a number of books.

Ed thrives on coming up with fresh ideas. Making a difference and turning one of those ideas into useful, working "things" is what floats Ed's boat.

Away from the crazy world of the Web, Ed has run the Edinburgh Marathon and abseiled down a lighthouse, raising thousands of pounds for charity. He captained his local Scottish rugby team for three seasons, winning the championship as top scorer and reaching the final of a national competition.

You may not know that Ed is the Dad from Jack Draws Anything (http://jackdrawsanything.com/) and the winner of the prestigious .net magazine Social Campaign of the Year (2011) award.

Ed lives in Corte Madera, California, USA (just 15 minutes from San Francisco) with the rest of Team Hendo: his amazing wife Rose and sidekicks Jack, Toby, and Noah.

Ed likes cake, bacon, cider, and talking about himself in the third person.

Rokesh Jankie graduated with a Masters degree in Computer Science from Leiden University, the Netherlands, in 1998. His field of specialization was Algorithms and NP-complete problems. Scheduling problems can be NP-complete, and that's the area he focused on. After that, he started working for the University of Leiden. He then went on to work with ORTEC consultants, Ponte Vecchio, and later, with Qualogy. At Qualogy, he used his experience thus far to set up a product. Qualogy works in the fields of Oracle and Java technologies. With the current set of technologies, interesting products can be delivered; that is QAFE (see www.qafe.com for more info).

The company that he works for now is specialized in Oracle and Java technologies. As head of the product development department and CTO of QAFE Inc., his focus is on the future of web application development. At the company, modern technologies (such as HTML5, Google APIs, AngularJS, NodeJS, and Java) are used, and close contact is kept with some excellent people at Google to make things work.

He has also reviewed the books *HTML5 Canvas Cookbook* by *Packt Publishing* and *Dart in Action* by *Manning Publications Co.*

I'm very honored and grateful that I was contacted to review this book. Savio Jose gave me the opportunity to review the book. It always feels good to be part of the next big thing on the Web (HTML5, CSS3, and JavaScript) in this way and for this particular topic. The future of web applications looks very promising.

www.PacktPub.com

Support files, eBooks, discount offers and more

You might want to visit www.PacktPub.com for support files and downloads related to your book.

Did you know that Packt offers eBook versions of every book published, with PDF and ePub files available? You can upgrade to the eBook version at www.PacktPub.com and as a print book customer, you are entitled to a discount on the eBook copy. Get in touch with us at service@packtpub.com for more details.

At www.PacktPub.com, you can also read a collection of free technical articles, sign up for a range of free newsletters and receive exclusive discounts and offers on Packt books and eBooks.

http://PacktLib.PacktPub.com

Do you need instant solutions to your IT questions? PacktLib is Packt's online digital book library. Here, you can access, read and search across Packt's entire library of books.

Why Subscribe?

- ► Fully searchable across every book published by Packt
- ► Copy and paste, print and bookmark content
- ► On demand and accessible via web browser

Free Access for Packt account holders

If you have an account with Packt at www.PacktPub.com, you can use this to access PacktLib today and view nine entirely free books. Simply use your login credentials for immediate access.

Table of Contents

Preface

HTML5 and CSS3 Responsive Web Design Cookbook gives developers a new toolbox for staying connected with this new skillset. Using the clear instructions given in the book, you can apply and create responsive applications and give your web project the latest design and development advantages for mobile devices. Using real-world examples, this book presents practical how-to recipes for site enhancements with a lighthearted, easy-to-understand tone. Gain a real understanding of Responsive Web Design and how to create an optimized display for an array of devices. The topics in this book include responsive elements and media, responsive typography, responsive layouts, using media queries, utilizing modern responsive frameworks, developing mobile-first web applications, optimizing responsive content, and achieving unobtrusive interaction using JavaScript and jQuery. Each recipe features actual lines of code that you can apply.

What this book covers

Chapter 1, Responsive Elements and Media, covers the creation of elements that optimize to mobile devices or desktop computers.

Chapter 2, Responsive Typography, teaches you about using fluid typography, creating cool text effects, and creating text that stands out on your screen through the HTML5 canvas and CSS3.

Chapter 3, Responsive Layout, teaches you how to create responsive layouts that you can really use in your projects. You will learn about using viewport and media queries to make your web project respond to different viewport sizes and types.

Chapter 4, Using Responsive Frameworks, teaches you how to use new frameworks to deploy responsive sites with the latest responsive methods and interactions quickly and reliably, and how to turn old static frameworks into responsive ones.

Chapter 5, Making Mobile-first Web Applications, teaches you how to make mobile web versions of your web application, which are optimized to be mobile-first, with jQuery Mobile, and how to optimize for the desktop viewport.

Chapter 6, Optimizing Responsive Content, teaches you about getting and using all the tools you need to build and test your responsive web project.

Chapter 7, Unobtrusive JavaScript, teaches you how to write JavaScript that lives out of your web page so that you can have thoughtful, responsive interactions for different devices.

What you need for this book

You will need an IDE (integrated development environment); NetBeans or Eclipse is recommended (there are instructions on how to get one inside), image editing software such as Photoshop or GIMP, a web host, and a local web server such as Apache or a local hosting application such as XAMPP or MAMPP.

Who this book is for

This book, for all of today's wireless Internet devices, is for web developers seeking innovative techniques that deliver fast, intuitive interfacing with the latest mobile Internet devices.

Conventions

In this book, you will find a number of styles of text that distinguish between different kinds of information. Here are some examples of these styles, and an explanation of their meaning.

Code words in text, database table names, folder names, filenames, file extensions, pathnames, dummy URLs, user input, and Twitter handles are shown as follows: " The `height: auto` property acts to preserve the aspect ratio of the image."

A block of code is set as follows:

```
<p class="text">Loremipsum dolor sit amet…</p>
<div class="img-wrap">
  <img alt="robots image" class="responsive" src="robots.jpg">
  <p>Loremipsum dolor sit amet</p>
</div>
```

When we wish to draw your attention to a particular part of a code block, the relevant lines or items are set in bold:

```
<!DOCTYPE HTML>
<html>
    <head>
        <style>
    .rotate {
/* Chrome, Safari 3.1+*/
-webkit-transform: rotate(-90deg);
```

```
/* Firefox 3.5-15 */
-moz-transform: rotate(-90deg);
/* IE9 */
-ms-transform: rotate(-90deg);
/* Opera 10.50-12*/
-o-transform: rotate(-90deg);
/* IE */
transform: rotate(-90deg);
}
        </style>
    </head>
    <body >
        <p class="rotate">I think, therefore I am </p>
    </body>
</html>
```

New terms and **important words** are shown in bold. Words that you see on the screen, in menus or dialog boxes for example, appear in the text like this: "However, what I really want is a large image, so I click on **Search tools**, and then on **Any Size**, which I change to **Large**.".

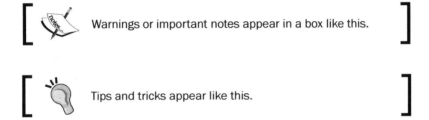

Warnings or important notes appear in a box like this.

Tips and tricks appear like this.

Reader feedback

Feedback from our readers is always welcome. Let us know what you think about this book— what you liked or may have disliked. Reader feedback is important for us to develop titles that you really get the most out of.

To send us general feedback, simply send an e-mail to feedback@packtpub.com, and mention the book title via the subject of your message.

If there is a topic that you have expertise in and you are interested in either writing or contributing to a book, see our author guide on www.packtpub.com/authors.

Customer support

Now that you are the proud owner of a Packt book, we have a number of things to help you to get the most from your purchase.

Downloading the example code

You can download the example code files for all Packt books you have purchased from your account at `http://www.packtpub.com`. If you purchased this book elsewhere, you can visit `http://www.packtpub.com/support` and register to have the files e-mailed directly to you.

Errata

Although we have taken every care to ensure the accuracy of our content, mistakes do happen. If you find a mistake in one of our books—maybe a mistake in the text or the code—we would be grateful if you would report this to us. By doing so, you can save other readers from frustration and help us improve subsequent versions of this book. If you find any errata, please report them by visiting `http://www.packtpub.com/submit-errata`, selecting your book, clicking on the **errata submission form** link, and entering the details of your errata. Once your errata are verified, your submission will be accepted and the errata will be uploaded on our website, or added to any list of existing errata, under the Errata section of that title. Any existing errata can be viewed by selecting your title from `http://www.packtpub.com/support`.

Piracy

Piracy of copyright material on the Internet is an ongoing problem across all media. At Packt, we take the protection of our copyright and licenses very seriously. If you come across any illegal copies of our works, in any form, on the Internet, please provide us with the location address or website name immediately so that we can pursue a remedy.

Please contact us at `copyright@packtpub.com` with a link to the suspected pirated material.

We appreciate your help in protecting our authors, and our ability to bring you valuable content.

Questions

You can contact us at `questions@packtpub.com` if you are having a problem with any aspect of the book, and we will do our best to address it.

1

Responsive Elements and Media

In this chapter, you will learn about:

- ► Resizing an image using percent width
- ► Responsive images using the cookie and JavaScript
- ► Making your video respond to your screen width
- ► Resizing an image using media queries
- ► Changing your navigation with media queries
- ► Making a responsive padding based on size
- ► Making a CSS3 button glow for a loading element

Introduction

The responsiveness website design and media is one of the most exciting things to happen to web development since ASCII art appeared on bulletin boards back when I was a school boy. The new cool features of HTML5, CSS3, and jQuery have brought new life to the old web in ways that have brought back the fun and really gets the Web audiences excited for using your applications. This chapter contains several recipes that will help you create responsive HTML elements and different media.

Some recipes are easy and some are more challenging. All of the code used for the **responsive web design** elements is provided inside the book, therefore nothing inside will be impossible to accomplish. Each and all of the responsive web design recipes will help you optimize your website's presentation to create an amazing responsive web experience for your audience no matter what device type or size you are using.

Resizing an image using percent width

This method relies on client-side coding for resizing a large image. It serves only one image to the client and asks it to render the image according to the size of the browser's window. This is usually the preferable method when you are confident that the clients have the bandwidth to download the image without causing the page to load slowly.

Getting ready

First you will need an image. To find a high-quality image, use Google Image Search. A search for `robots`, for example, the search gives me 158,000,000 results, which is pretty good. However, what I really want is a large image, so I click on **Search tools**, and then click on **Any Size**, which I change to **Large**. I still have 4,960,000 images to choose from.

The image should be resized to match the largest scale viewable. Open it in your image-editing software. If you don't have an image-editing software already, there are many free ones, go get one. Gimp is a powerful image-editing software and it's open source, or free to download. Go to `http://www.gimp.org` to get this powerful open source image-editing software.

How to do it...

Once you have your image-editing software, open the image in it and change the image's width to 300px. Save your new image and then move or upload the image to your web directory.

Your HTML should contain your image and some text to demonstrate the responsive effect. If you do not have time to write your life story, you can go back to the Internet and get some sample text from an Ipsum generator. Go to `http://www.lipsum.com` and generate a paragraph of Ipsum text.

```
<p class="text">Loremipsum dolor sit amet...</p>
<div class="img-wrap" >
    <img alt="robots image" class="responsive" src="robots.jpg" >
    <p>Loremipsum dolor sit amet</p>
</div>
```

Your CSS should include a class for your paragraph and one for your image and an image wrapper. Float the paragraph to the left and give it a width of `60%`, and the image wrapper with a width of `40%`.

```
p.text {
    float:left;
```

```
        width:60%;
    }
    div.img-wrap{
        float:right;
        width:40%;
    }
```

This creates a fluid layout, but does not yet do anything to create a responsive image. The image will stay at a static width of 300px until you add the following CSS. Then, add a new class to the CSS for the image. Assign it a `max-width` value of `100%`. This allows the width to adjust to the browser width changes. Next, add a dynamic `height` property to the class.

```
    img.responsive {
        max-width: 100%;
        height: auto;
    }
```

This creates an image that responds to the browser window's width with an optimized version of that image for the audience.

How it works...

The `responsive` property of the image CSS forces it to take 100 percent of its parent element. When the parent element's width changes, the image changes to fill in that width. The `height: auto` property acts to preserve the aspect ratio of the image.

See also

▶ The *Responsive images using the cookie and JavaScript* recipe
▶ The *Making a responsive padding based on size* recipe

Responsive images using the cookie and JavaScript

A responsive image's width can be delivered through complicated server logic. Sometimes because of the requirements you cannot achieve the desired results through the easiest method. The percent-width method relies on the client side for image resizing of a large image file. This method provides a server-side delivery of the properly sized image you request. It may reduce the server load and bandwidth and help you with long loading, if you are concerned with slow loading affecting the performance of your website.

Getting ready

These methods require your server to perform some sort of logic function on it. Firstly, it requires PHP on your server. It also requires you to create three different sized versions of the image and serve them to the client as requested.

How to do it...

The JavaScript is simple. It creates a cookie based on your device's screen dimensions. When the client makes a request to the server for an image, it fires the PHP code to deliver the appropriate image.

```
<script >
    document.cookie = "screen_dimensions=" + screen.width + "x" +
screen.height;
</script>
```

Now, on your server, create an `images` folder in the web directory and create a PHP file (`index.php`) with the following code in it:

```php
<?php
$screen_w = 0;
$screen_h = 0;
$img = $_SERVER['QUERY_STRING'];

if (file_exists($img)) {

   // Get screen dimensions from the cookie
   if (isset($_COOKIE['screen_dimensions'])) {
     $screen = explode('x', $_COOKIE['screen_dimensions']);
     if (count($screen)==2) {
       $screen_w = intval($screen[0]);
       $screen_h = intval($screen[1]);
     }
   }
}
```

```
    if ($screen_width> 0) {

      $theExt = pathinfo($img, PATHINFO_EXTENSION);

      // for Low resolution screen
      if ($screen_width>= 1024) {
        $output = substr_replace($img, '-med', -strlen($theExt)-1,
      }

      // for Medium resolution screen
      else if ($screen_width<= 800) {
        $output = substr_replace($img, '-low', -strlen($theExt)-1, 0);
      }

      // check if file exists
      if (isset($output) &&file_exists($output)) {
        $img = $output;
      }
    }

    // return the image file;
    readfile($img);
  }

?>
```

Now with your image-editing software, open your large image and create two smaller versions of it. If the original version is 300px, then make the next two copies 200px and 100px. Then, name them `robot.png`, `robot-med.png`, and `robot-low.png` respectively. Upload these three images into the `images` folder.

Last, but not least, put the following HTML file in your server's document root:

```
<!doctype html>
<html>
    <head>
        <title>Responsive Images</title>
        <meta charset="utf-8">
        <script>
    document.cookie = "device_dimensions=" + screen.width + "x" +
screen.height;
        </script>
    </head>
    <body>
        <img alt="robot image" src="images/index.php?robot.png">
    </body>
</html>
```

You can see the recipe in action in the following screenshot:

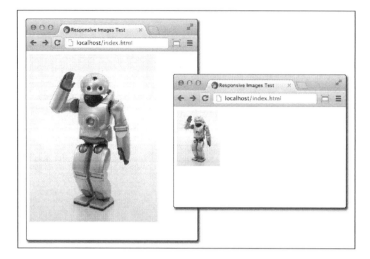

While this method is limited to delivering a specific image for each screen size, and is not fluidly dynamic, it does provide the same functionality on the server side as a CSS media query. You can style the served image with CSS or animate it with JavaScript. It can be used with a combination of methods to provide responsive content.

The code for this recipe was originally created by the clever folks at `http://www.html.it/articoli/responsive-images-con-i-cookie/`.

How it works...

The HTML file first creates a cookie describing your device's screen dimensions. When the image element calls the PHP file it works like an `include` statement in PHP. The PHP file first checks for the file to exist, then reads the cookie for the screen width, and delivers the appropriate-sized version of the image.

Making your video respond to your screen width

The streaming of video can also be responsive. You can easily embed an HTML5 video in your page and make it responsive. The `video` tag easily supports using a percent width. However, it requires that you have the video source on your website's host. If you have this available, this is easy.

```
<style>
video {
```

```css
        max-width: 100%;
        height: auto;
    }
</style>
```

```html
<video width="320" height="240" controls="controls">
    <source src="movie.mp4" type="video/mp4">
    <source src="movie.ogg" type="video/ogg">
    Your browser does not support the video tag.
</video>
```

However, using a video-hosting site, such as YouTube or Vimeo, has many advantages over hosting it yourself. First, there is the bandwidth issue, you may have bandwidth or disk space limits on your hosting server. Additionally, video-hosting sites make the upload conversion to a usable web video surprisingly easy, compared to using only your own resources.

Getting ready

The video-hosting sites allow you to embed an iFrame or object code snippet in your page to stream the video on your site. This won't work inside the `video` tag. So, to make it responsive, there is a more complex, but still easy method.

How to do it...

Wrap the video-source snippet in an HTML containing the `div` element and give it a 50 to 60 percent padding on the bottom and relative positions. Then give its child element, the video iFrame object, a `100%` width and `100%` height, and an `absolute` position. This makes the iFrame object completely fill in the parent element.

The following is the HTML code that uses an `iframe` tag to get a video from Vimeo:

```html
<div class="video-wrap">
    <iframe src="http://player.vimeo.com/video/52948373?badge=0"
width = "800" height= "450" frameborder="0"></iframe>
</div>
```

The following is the HTML code using the older YouTube object with markup:

```html
<div class="video-wrap">
    <object width="800" height="450">
        <param name="movie" value="http://www.youtube.com/v/
b803LeMGkCA?version=3&amp;hl=en_US">
        </param>
        <param name="allowFullScreen" value="true"></param>
```

```
            <param name="allowscriptaccess" value="always"></param>
            <embed src="http://www.youtube.com/v/
b803LeMGkCA?version=3&amp;hl=en_US" type="application/x-shockwave-
flash" width="560" height="315" allowscriptaccess="always"
allowfullscreen="true">
            </embed>
        </object>
</div>
```

Both video types use the same CSS:

```
.video-wrap {
    position:relative;
    padding-bottom: 55%;
    padding-top: 30px;
    height: 0;
    overflow:hidden;
}
.video-wrap iframe,
.video-wrap object,
.video-wrap embed {
    position:absolute;
    top:0;
    width:100%;
    height:100%;
}
```

You might not want the video to take up the entire width of the page. In this case, you can limit the width of the video using `width` and `max-width`. Then, wrap the `video-wrap` element with the another `div` element and assign a fixed `width` value and `max-width:100%`.

```
<div class="video-outer-wrap">
    <div class="video-wrap">
        <iframe src="http://player.vimeo.com/video/6284199?title=0&b
yline=0&portrait=0" width="800" height="450" frameborder="0">
        </iframe>
    </div>
</div>

.video-outer-wrap {
    width: 500px;
    max-width:100%;
}
```

This recipe will work on all modern browsers.

How it works...

This method is called Intrinsic Ratios for Videos, created by Thierry Koblentz on A List Apart. You wrap the video inside an element that has an intrinsic aspect ratio, and then give the video an absolute position. This locks the aspect ratio, while allowing the size to be fluid.

Resizing an image using media queries

The media query is another useful and highly customizable method for responsive images. This is different than responsive fluid width achieved by the percent-width method. Your design may require some specific image widths for different screen size ranges and a fluid width would break your design.

Getting ready

This method only requires one image, and makes the client's browser resize the image instead of the server.

How to do it...

The HTML code is simple, using the standard image tag, create an image element, as follows:

```
<img alt="robot image" src="robot.png">
```

To start with a simple version, create a media query that will detect the browser window's size and deliver a larger image for browser screens larger than `1024px`, and a smaller image for smaller browser windows. First the media query, it looks for the media type `screen`, and then the screen size. When the media query is satisfied the browser will render the CSS inside the brackets.

```
@media screen and ( max-width: 1024px ) {...}
@media screen and ( min-width: 1025px ) {...}
```

Now, add a class to your image tag. The class will respond differently in different media queries, as shown in the following code line:

```
<img alt="robot image" src="robot.png" class="responsive"/>
```

Adding the CSS class to each media query with a different size will make the browser render the desired image size to each differently sized browser window. The media query can coexist with other CSS classes. Then, outside of the media queries, add a CSS class for the image with `height:auto`. This will work for both media queries with only adding one line of CSS.

```
@media screen and ( max-width: 1024px ) {
img.responsive { width: 200px; }
```

```
}
@media screen and ( min-width: 1025px) {
img.responsive { width: 300px;}
}
img.responsive { height: auto; }
```

To make the image respond to multiple ranges you can combine the `max-width` and `min-width` media queries. To specify an image size for browser windows, sized between `1024px` and `1280px`, add a media query for screen, `1024px` as `min-width`, and `1280px` as `max-width`.

```
@media screen and ( max-width: 1024px ) {
img.responsive { width: 200px; }
}
@media screen and ( min-width:1025px ) and ( max-width: 1280px ) {
img.responsive { width: 300px; }
}
@media screen and ( min-width: 1081px ) {
img.responsive { width: 400px; }
}
img.responsive { height: auto; }
```

You can specify many different image sizes for many different browser window sizes with the media query method.

How it works...

The media query of CSS3 gives your CSS logical conditions based on the browser's viewport properties, and can render different styles based on the browser's window properties. This recipe takes advantage of this by setting a different image width for many different browser's window sizes. Thus delivering a responsive image size, you can control with a high degree of granularity.

Changing your navigation with media queries

The media query can do more than just resizing images. You can use the media query to deliver a much more dynamic web page to your viewers. You can display a responsive menu based on different screen sizes using media queries.

Getting ready

To make a responsive menu system, using two different menus we will display a dynamic menu for three different browser window sizes.

How to do it...

For the smaller browser windows, and especially for mobile devices and tablets, create a simple `select` menu that only takes up a small amount of vertical space. This menu uses an HTML `form` element for the navigation options that fires a JavaScript code to load the new page on selection.

```
<div class="small-menu">
     <form>
          <select name="URL" onchange="window.location.href=this.form.
URL.options[this.form.URL.selectedIndex].value">
               <option value="blog.html">My Blog</option>
               <option value="home.html">My Home Page</option>
               <option value="tutorials.html">My Tutorials</option>
          </select>
     <form>
</div>
```

For the larger browser window sizes, create a simple `ul` list element that can be styled through CSS. This menu will receive a different layout and look from the different media queries. This menu is added to the same page following the `select` menu:

```
<div class="large-menu">
     <ul>
          <li>
               <a href="blog.html">My Blog</a>
          </li>
          <li>
               <a href="home.html">My Home Page</a>
          </li>
          <li>
               <a href="tutorials.html">My Tutorials</a>
          </li>
     </ul>
</div>
```

To make the menu responsive, create a media query for the target browser window sizes. For browser windows smaller than `800px`, the CSS will display only the `select` form inside the `div` element with the `small-menu` class, for all larger browser windows, the CSS will display the `ul` list inside the `div` element with the `large-menu` class. This creates an effect where the page will shift between menus when the browser window crosses width of `801px`.

```
@media screen and ( max-width: 800px ) {
.small-menu { display:inline; }
.large-menu { display:none; }
```

```
}
@media screen and ( min-width: 801px ) and ( max-width: 1024px ) {
.small-menu { display:none; }.
.large-menu { display:inline; }
}
@media screen and ( min-width: 1025px ) {
.small-menu { display:none; }
.large-menu { display:inline; }
}
```

For the larger screen sizes, you can use the same `ul` list and use the media query even further to deliver a different menu by simply switching out the CSS and using the same HTML.

For the medium-sized menu, use CSS to display the list items as a horizontal list, as shown in the following code snippet:

```
.large-menu ul{
    list-style-type:none;
}
.large-menu ul li {
    display:inline;
}
```

This turns the list into a horizontal list. We want this version of the navigation to appear on the medium-sized browser windows. Place it inside the media query ranging between `801px` and `1024px`, as shown in the following code snippet:

```
@media screen and ( min-width: 801px ) and (max-width: 1024px ) {
    .small-menu {
        display:none;
    }
.large-menu {
        display:inline;
    }
.large-menu ul {
        list-style-type:none;
    }
.large-menu ul li {
        display:inline;
    }
}
@media screen and (min-width: 1025px ) {
.small-menu {
        display:none;
    }
```

```
    .large-menu {
        display:inline;
    }
}
```

To further utilize the responsive navigation elements in the best way possible, we want the menu list version to move to a different layout location when the screen's width changes. For the middle width, `801px` to `1024px`, the menu stays on top of the page and has a `100%` width. When the screen is wider than `1025px`, the menu will float to the left-hand side of its parent element. Add to the `801px` to `1024px` media query a `100%` width to the `large-menu` class, and to the `1025px` media query, add a `20%` width and a `float:left` value to the `large-menu` class.

To fill out the page we will also add a paragraph of text wrapped in a `div` element. You can go back to the Lorem Ipsum text generator to create filler text (`http://lipsum.com/`). In the medium-width media query give the element containing the paragraph a `100%` width. In the largest media query, give the element containing the paragraph a width of `80%` and float it to the right-hand side of its parent element.

```
<div class="small-menu">
    <form>
        <select name="URL" onchange="window.location.href=this.form.
URL.options[this.form.URL.selectedIndex].value">
            <option value="blog.html">My Blog</option>
            <option value="home.html">My Home Page</option>
            <option value="tutorials.html">My Tutorials</option>
        </select>
    <form>
</div>

<div class="large-menu">
    <ul>
        <li>
            <a href="blog.html">My Blog</a>
        </li>
        <li>
            <a href="home.html">My Home Page</a>
        </li>
        <li>
            <a href="tutorials.html">My Tutorials</a>
        </li>
    </ul>
</div>

<div class="content">
    <p>Loremipsum dolor sitamet, consecteturadipiscingelit...</p>
</div>
```

And your style should look as shown in following code snippet:

```
<style>
@media screen and ( max-width: 800px ) {
    .small-menu {
        display: inline;
    }
    .large-menu {
        display: none;
    }
}
@media screen and ( min-width: 801px ) and ( max-width: 1024px ) {
    .small-menu {
        display: none;
    }
    .large-menu {
        display:inline;
        width: 100%;
    }
    .large-menu ul {
        list-style-type: none;
    }
    .large-menu ul li {
        display: inline;
    }
    .content: {
        width: 100%;
    }
}
@media screen and ( min-width: 1025px ) {
    .small-menu {
        display: none;
    }
    .large-menu {
        display: inline;
        float: left;
        width: 20%;
    }
    .content{
        float: right;
        width: 80%;
    }
}
</style>
```

The final result is a page with three different versions of the navigation. Your audience will be amazed when given an optimized version of the menu for each particular browser window size. You can see the navigation elements in all their glory in the following screenshot:

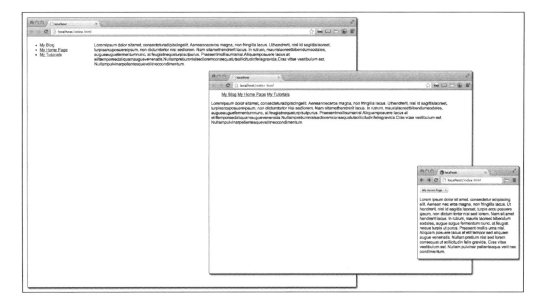

How it works...

Each version of the navigation utilizes the media query CSS3 property to maximize the space available for the menu and the content. In the smallest window, below `1024px`, the navigation is packed neatly inside a `select` form element. The medium window, ranging from `1025px` to `1280px`, the navigation is inline and spans across the top of the page, and is followed by the content. Finally, in the widest browser widths, the menu floats on the left-hand side and takes only 20 percent of the horizontal screen space, while the content is maximized on the remaining 80 percent (right-hand side) of the wide-browser window. This technique requires more planning and effort, but is well worth it to deliver the best possible viewing to your audience.

Making a responsive padding based on size

To complement a responsive width image element, relative padding can be added. With a static width padding, the image padding may appear too thick in smaller browser windows and overcrowd any other elements nearby, or may push the image off the screen.

Getting ready

A good place to start is with some understanding of the calculation of the box model properties. The total width an object takes is its actual width plus its padding, border, and margin on both sides, or *2 x (margin + border + padding) + content = total width*.

How to do it...

For an image that is 200px wide in its normal non-responsive state, your typical padding may be 8px, therefore using the previous box model, the formula can be framed as follows:

```
2 x ( 0 + 0 + 8px ) + 200px = 216px
```

To find the percentage of padding, divide the padding by the total width, `8 / 216 = 0.037%` rounded to `4%`.

We created this CSS and HTML earlier when we created the responsive percent-width image. Add to the image class a padding of `4%`.

```
<style>
p.text {
      float: left;
      width: 60%;
    }
div.img-wrap{
      float: right;
      margin: 0px;
      width: 38%;
    }
img.responsive {
      max-width: 100%;
      height: auto;
      padding: 4%;
    }
</style>

<p class="text">ipsum dolor sit amet, consecteturadi...</p>
<div class="img-wrap">
      <img alt="robot image" class="responsive" src="robot.png">
      <p>ipsum dolor sit amet, consecteturadipiscingelit...</p>
</div>
```

To help you see the actual padding width change as you change the browser window's size, add a background color (`background-color: #cccccc;`) to your image CSS.

How it works...

The image padding set at 100 percent will stick to the edge of its parent element. As the parent element size changes, the image padding adjusts accordingly. If you have done your box model math properly, your layout will successfully respond to your browser window's changing width.

Making a CSS3 button glow for a loading element

Your website, like many others, may cater to impatient people. If your site has a submitable form, your users may find themselves clicking the "submit" button a number of times impatiently if your page does not load the new content quick enough. This can be a problem when it causes multiple form submissions with the same data.

Getting ready

You can stop this behavior by adding some simple visual cues that tell the user something is happening behind the scenes and to be a little patient. If it's a little bit flashy, it might even bring a little sunshine into their otherwise hurried lives. This recipe does not require any images, we are going to create a handsome gradient submit button using CSS only. You may want to pause and go get a cup of coffee, as this is the longest recipe in this chapter.

How to do it...

You can start by creating a form with some text boxes and a submit button. Then, make the form really cool, use the HTML5 placeholder property for the label. Even with the placeholders, the form is pretty boring.

Note that this is not yet supported in Internet Explorer 9.

```
<h1>My Form<h1>
<form>
    <ul>
        <li>
          <input type="text" placeholder="Enter your first name"/>
        </li>
        <li>
          <input type="text" placeholder="Enter your last name"/>
        </li>
    </ul>
<input type="submit" name="Submit" value="Submit">
</form>
```

By adding CSS properties we can start giving the button some life:

```
input[type="submit"] {
    color: white;
    padding: 5px;
    width: 68px;
    height: 28px;
    border-radius: 5px;
    border: 1px;
    font-weight: bold;
    border: 1px groove #7A7A7A;
}
```

This is illustrated in the following screenshot:

The button can become even more shiny when we add a CSS3 gradient effect. To accomplish this, there must be a different line of CSS for each browser rendering engine: Opera, Internet Explorer, WebKit (Chrome and Safari), and Firefox. You can add as many gradient shifts as you like, simply by adding a `color` phase and the % location from the top, each shift separated by a comma, as shown in the following code snippet:

```
<style>
input[type="submit"] {
    background: -moz-linear-gradient(top, #0F97FF 0%, #97D2FF
8%,#0076D1 62%, #0076D1 63%, #005494 100%);
    background: -webkit-gradient(linear, left top, left bottom,
color-stop(0%,#0F97FF), color-stop(8%,#97D2FF)color-stop(50%,#0076D1),
color-stop(51%,#0076D1), color-stop(100%,#005494));
    background: -webkit-linear-gradient(top, #0F97FF 0%,#97D2FF
8%,#0076D1 62%,#0076D1 63%,#005494 100%);
    background: -o-linear-gradient(top, #0F97FF 0%,#97D2FF 8%,#0076D1
62%,#0076D1 63%,#005494 100%);
```

```
    background: -ms-linear-gradient(top, #0F97FF 0%,#97D2FF
8%,#0076D1 62%,#0076D1 63%,#005494 100%);
    background: linear-gradient(to bottom, #0F97FF
0%,#97D2FF 8%,#0076D1 62%,#0076D1 63%,#005494 100%);filter:
progid:DXImageTransform.Microsoft.gradient( startColorstr='#0f97ff',
endColorstr='#005494',GradientType=0 );
}
</style>
```

This effect is illustrated in the following screenshot:

Another effect can be added to the button by CSS, the `hover` effect. With this property, when the pointer moves over the button, it looks like it is being pressed in. The following CSS will help you add that dark border to the button:

```
input[type="submit"]:hover {
    border: 2px groove #7A7A7A;
}
```

This is displayed in the following screenshot:

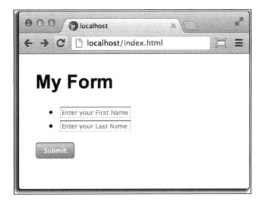

Using CSS3 Box Shadows and jQuery we can make a simple animation of a pulsing halo around the **Submit** button after you pushed it. Create an event listener with jQuery that listens for the button's `click` event, and on that `click` event a series of class changes on the form button element. The `partial-fade` class will be added by the script to the button element.

> Don't forget to add a link in your `head` tag to the jQuery source:
> ```
> <scriptsrc="http://code.jquery.com/jquery-latest.
> js"></script>
> ```

Then, insert the following script after the form closes:

```
<script >
//Submit Glow
$('input[type="submit"]').click(function() {
$(this).addClass('partial-fade');
    $(this).animate({
        opacity: 0.1
    }, 8).animate({
        opacity: 0.9
    }, 226).animate({
        opacity: .5
    }, 86);
    setTimeout(function () {
        $('input[type="submit"]').removeClass('partial-fade');
    }, 366).animate({
        opacity: 1
    }, 86);
});
</script>
```

To finish making the button glow when you click it, add the new class `partial-fade`, to your CSS file and give it a CSS3 Box Shadow Property, and change the border properties.

```
<style>
input[type="submit"].partial-fade {
    border-top: 1px solid #CFF !important;
    border-right: 1px solid #CCF !important;
    border-left: 1px solid #CCF !important;
    border-bottom: 1px solid #6CF !important;
    -webkit-box-shadow: 0 08px 0px #0F97FF, inset 0 0 20px rgba(37,
141, 220, 1);
    -moz-box-shadow: 0 0 8px 0px #0F97FF, inset 0 0 20px
rgba(37,141,220,1);
```

```
       box-shadow: 0 0 8px 0px #0F97FF, inset 0 0 20px rgba(37, 141,
  220, 1);
  }
  </style>
```

Now, the **Submit** button will give a flash of blue when pressed. The following screenshot shows the final product:

Whew! This button was a lot of work for such a small detail, but the details like this will really help make a great-looking website. This happens to be one of my favorite details to surprise my audience with.

How it works...

The CSS3 background gradient is an easy way to make a great-looking button consistently across browsers. The gradient is complicated and each browser currently requires its own line for CSS. You can control the gradient breakpoints by adding the percentage and colors manually. Adding box shadow, borders, and jQuery make fun effects on the button when the event is fired.

2

Responsive Typography

In this chapter, you will learn about:

- ▶ Creating fluid, responsive typography
- ▶ Making a text shadow with canvas
- ▶ Making an inner and outer shadow with canvas
- ▶ Rotating your text with canvas
- ▶ Rotating your text with CSS3
- ▶ Making 3D text with CSS3
- ▶ Adding texture to your text with CSS3 text masking
- ▶ Styling alternating rows with the nth positional pseudo class
- ▶ Adding characters before and after pseudo elements
- ▶ Making a button with a relative font size
- ▶ Adding a shadow to your font
- ▶ Curving a corner with border radius

Introduction

This chapter deals mostly with how to make responsive typography. You will learn recipes for optimizing your text for various types of device, as well as methods to embellish your typography. The technologies involved are simply CSS3 and HTML5's `canvas` element with JavaScript. With responsive typography, you can apply a number of exciting effects to your text.

When finished with this chapter, you should be armed with a number of techniques that will get you started on the road to making amazing responsive websites. These recipes cover the basics, but when combined together with some creativity, they will enable you to do some fantastic production.

Creating fluid, responsive typography

This recipe is a simple example of responsive typography. It will demonstrate the use of the new size unit REM. REM means Root EM. This simply means that the size of the font is relative to the root's font size, not the parent, as with the EM unit.

Getting ready

Without any further discussion, let's jump into this recipe. Go get some filler text from my favorite Ipsum generator (http://ipsum.com). Generate at least one paragraph and copy the text into your clipboard.

How to do it...

Now, paste the filler text into your HTML document and wrap it in a paragraph tag. Give the paragraph element class= "a", then make a copy and assign the new paragraph class="b", as shown in the following code snippet:

```
<p class="a">
    Lorem ipsum dolor sit amet, consectetur adipiscing elit.
<p>

<p class="b">
    ultricies ut viverra massa rutrum. Nunc pharetra, ipsum ut
    ullamcorper placerat,
<p>
```

Next, create a style for the base HTML font-size property, and then one for the static sized paragraph to compare the font size changes—similar to an experiment's control group:

```
html{font-size:12px;}
p.b{font-size:1rem;}
```

Next create two @media queries, one for orientation:portrait, and the second one for orientation:landscape. In the orientation:portrait media query, style the "a" class paragraph element with a font-size value of 3rem. And in the orientation:landscape media query, style the "a" class paragraph with the font-size value of 1rem.

```
@media screen and (orientation:portrait){
p.a{font-size:3rem;}
}
@media screen and (orientation:landscape){
p.a{font-size:1rem;}
}
```

Now when you resize your browser window from landscape to portrait mode, you will see the font size of the first paragraph goes from a ratio of 1:1 to the base size, to 3:1 of the base size. While this seems very simple, this recipe can be varied and built on to create a number of impressive responsive typography tricks.

How it works...

When your browser makes a request, the CSS3 `@media` query returns some conditional styles based on viewport's width. It loads or builds (rebuilds) on the fly for changes to the viewport's size. While not many in your audience are going to spend much time resizing your website in their browser, it is easy to spend too much time worrying about how your website shifts from one size to the next.

See also

▸   The *Making a button with a relative font size* recipe

Making a text shadow with canvas

HTML5 brings a new element to web design, the `<canvas>` element. This is used to create graphics on a web page on the fly using JavaScript.

Getting ready

The `<canvas>` element creates a rectangular area on your page. It dimensions default to 300px by 150px. You can specify different settings inside the JavaScript. The code in this recipe grows quickly, so you can get the whole code online at the Packt Publishing's website.

How to do it...

To begin, create a simple HTML page with a `<canvas>` element:

```
<!DOCTYPE HTML>
<html>
    <head>

    </head>
    <body>
            <canvas id="thecanvas"></canvas>
    </body>
</html>
```

The JavaScript gets the `canvas` element from the DOM.

```
var canvas = document.getElementById('thecanvas');
```

It then calls the `getContext()` method. The `getContext('2d')` method is the built-in HTML5 object. It has a number of methods to draw text, shapes, images, and more.

```
var ctx = canvas.getContext('2d');
```

Next, start drawing the text within the JavaScript. Here, we create a code to draw the horizontal and vertical shadow offsets, the blur, and the color of the shadow.

```
ctx.shadowOffsetX = 2;
ctx.shadowOffsetY = 2;
ctx.shadowBlur = 2;
ctx.shadowColor = "rgba(0, 0, 0, 0.5)";
```

The text and its properties is written in the JavaScript here, but can be passed in as a variable from the DOM:

```
ctx.font = "20px Times New Roman";
ctx.fillStyle = "Black";
ctx.fillText("This is the canvas", 5, 30);
```

Back in the HTML, add the `onload="drawCanvas();"` script command to the `body` element. When the page loads, the JavaScript fires and draws the text and its shadow onto the canvas. This is illustrated in the following screenshot:

How it works...

Without getting too deep into the gears of JavaScript, the `canvas` element provides a place for the designer to script some content directly to the page on page load. The `body` element's `onload="drawCanvas();"` command fires the JavaScript, which draws the content onto the canvas.

See also

▸   The *Rotate your text with canvas* recipe

Making an inner and outer shadow with canvas

This recipe also uses `canvas` and JavaScript to draw the text and the effects in your browser. There is no direct method to make an inner-glow or inset-shadow effect using `canvas`, however, using the stroke method, you can simulate an inner shadow in your text.

Getting ready

This recipe starts with some already-written code. You can download this from Packt Publishing's website. It is also the same code you created in the recipe, *Making a text shadow with canvas*. This code should be run on your local computer without any special web server. You can get the whole code online at the book's website.

How to do it...

To begin, create a simple HTML page with a `<canvas>` element.

```
<html>
  <head>

  </head>
  <body>
    <canvas id="thecanvas"></canvas>
  </body>
</html>
```

The JavaScript gets the `canvas` element from the DOM.

```
var canvas = document.getElementById('thecanvas');
```

It then calls the `getContext()` method. The `getContext('2d')` method is the built-in HTML5 object. It has a number of methods to draw text, shapes, images, and more.

```
var context = canvas.getContext('2d');
```

This script uses multiple effects combined to make an inner and outer shadow. You add a drop shadow and two different outlines. First, add a drop shadow to the top-left part and make it black with a `context.shadowBlur` value of 2. Building on that, after `context.fillText`, add `context.strokeStyle` and `context.strokeText` to the canvas context.

```
context.shadowOffsetX = -1;
context.shadowOffsetY = -1;
context.shadowBlur = 2;
context.shadowColor = "#888888";
context.textAlign = "left";
context.font = "33px Times New Roman";
context.fillStyle = "#666";
context.fillText("This is the Canvas", 0, 50);
context.strokeStyle = "#555";
context.strokeText("This is the canvas", 2, 50);
context.linewidth = 2;
```

Instead of a raised look, the text appears to be beveled in and has an inner glow or shadow effect. The effect is displayed in the following screenshot:

How it works...

As stated in the beginning of this recipe, there is no true direct method to make an inner shadow in canvas, but there are ways to use the `context.fillText` and `context.strokeStyle` methods together that will create something that sufficiently looks like an inner shadow.

Rotating your text with canvas

The HTML5 canvas methods can do more than just coloring the text or adding drop shadows. You can also use it to move or manipulate the objects in the canvas area. In this recipe, we will rotate the objects in the canvas.

Getting ready

This recipe builds on top of the previous recipes. If you skipped them, that's okay, you can go back to the previous recipe to refer to the complete code.

How to do it...

Once you have your previous recipe's canvas set up, the basic steps for rotation are easy. Add a `rotate` method to the beginning of the function:

```
context.rotate(Math.PI/4,0,0);
```

You will probably notice that the text rotated right off of the canvas. What happened? The `rotate` method rotates the entire canvas and is not aware of what is in it.

The canvas has a small default size of 300px by 150px. Changing the element's size attributes will not affect the canvas size, but distorts the objects drawn on it. To change the size of the canvas and the objects drawn, add the `canvas.width` and `canvas.height` properties in the JavaScript:

```
canvas.width=250;
canvas.height=250;
```

In addition, because the canvas rotates entirely itself, and not the text rotating about an origin, the text location will need to be repositioned to desired location. In this case, change the object offset of the fill and the stroke:

```
context.fillText("This is the Canvas", 140, 1);
context.strokeText("This is the Canvas ", 140, 1);
```

This is depicted in the following screenshot:

How it works...

The JavaScript uses the `rotate` method to rotate the whole `canvas` element and everything drawn inside it. It requires a small amount of forethought when using the `rotate` method in the canvas. It is complex, but is the perfect tool to use in large responsive web projects.

See also

▶ The *Rotate your text with CSS3* recipe

Rotating your text with CSS3

CSS3 provides an easy way to rotate your text. The `transform:rotate` property is easy to implement and provides a simple solution when the project does not require the complexity of the canvas.

Getting ready

Write a line of text in your HTML document. Brace yourself; you are about to rotate it with CSS3.

How to do it...

Wrap the text in a paragraph tag element:

```
<p class="rotate">I think, therefore I am</p>
```

Then, add the CSS `transform` property to rotate the text. Each browser renders this differently, so each will need its own unique `transform` property. However, each will use the `transform` property's subproperty `rotate`, followed by the degrees of rotation, as shown in the following code snippet:

```
<!DOCTYPE HTML>
<html>
    <head>
        <style>
    .rotate {
/* Chrome, Safari 3.1+*/
-webkit-transform: rotate(-90deg);
/* Firefox 3.5-15 */
-moz-transform: rotate(-90deg);
/* IE9 */
-ms-transform: rotate(-90deg);
/* Opera 10.50-12*/
-o-transform: rotate(-90deg);
/* IE */
transform: rotate(-90deg);
}
        </style>
    </head>
    <body >
        <p class="rotate">I think, therefore I am </p>
    </body>
</html>
```

How it works...

The `transform` property applies a 2D or 3D transformation to an element. Other property changes available are `move`, `skew`, and `perspective`.

See also

▶ The *Rotate your text with canvas* recipe

Making 3D text with CSS3

In previous recipes, we created a drop shadow, bevel, and an inner shadow, using the `canvas` element. With CSS3, we can do this to make your text really stand out. Using the CSS3 `text-shadow` property, we can make your text look as if it is jutting out of the screen towards your viewer.

Getting ready

If you would like to skip ahead, you can get the code online at Packt Publishing's website. Otherwise, if you are the learning-by-doing type, let's make our 3D text. We create the 3D effect by using a combination of CSS3 shadow effects.

How to do it...

In your IDE, create a new HTML document with only a header in the body. Add a `style` section to the `head` tag and assign the header the property, `color:#f0f0f0;`, as shown in the following code snippet:

```
<style>
     h1{ color: #f0f0f0;}
</style>
```

Now add to it a series of seven increasing-decreasing X- and Y- positioned `text-shadow` properties, from `0px 0px0px #666`, to `-6px -6px 0px #666;`.

```
text-shadow: 0px 0px0px #666,
-1px -1px 0px #666,
-2px -2px 0px #666,
-3px -3px 0px #666,
-4px -4px 0px #666,
-5px -5px 0px #666,
-6px -6px 0px #000,
```

Your header now leaps off the screen. Well, almost! To make sure it really pops off the screen, let's give it some more effect. When building any 3D objects on a screen, it is important to give consistent lighting and shadows. Since this text rises above, it needs a shadow.

Add another series of six X- and Y- positioned `text-shadow` properties, only this time give them positive values and a lighter color (`color:#ccc;`).

```
1px 1px 5px #ccc,
 2px 2px 5px #ccc,
 3px 3px 5px #ccc,
```

```
4px  4px  5px  #ccc,
5px  5px5px  #ccc,
6px  6px  5px  #ccc;
```

The drop shadow makes sense, but it still looks a bit fake, well let's take it to another level; let's blur and darken the elements on the background. The third number in your `text-shadow` property creates the blur, so add an increasing blur of 0, 0, 1, 1, 2, 3, and 5, as shown in the following code. Also, change the colors to grow darker as you go back: `#888`, `#777`, `#666`, `#555`, `#444`, `#333`, and `#000`.

```
text-shadow:0px  0px0px  #888,
-1px  -1px  0px  #777,
-2px  -2px  1px  #666,
-3px  -3px  1px  #555,
-4px  -4px  2px  #444,
-5px  -5px  3px  #333,
-6px  -6px  4px  #000,
```

Now your header has a truly realistic 3D effect. The effect illustrated in the following screenshot:

How it works...

Play around and experiment with variations of this recipe for some very exciting typographic effects. CSS3 brings a whole new level of excitement and depth to typographic design that has always been difficult to achieve, and does it well.

The `text-shadow` property can handle numerous shadow properties. Therefore, you can stack them on top of each other in an increasing distance away from your text. This creates the 3D effect on your text.

Adding texture to your text with text masking

CSS3 also gives you the awesome power of adding an image mask texture to your text with an image. This effect was previously only achievable by creating a static image of your text with an image-editing software.

Getting ready

You'll need an image to use as the texture mask. Using an image-editing software, create a new image with an alpha channel. If you do not have an image-editing software that can create a PNG with alpha channels, you can download an open source, free image-editing software GIMP at http://www.gimp.org. To create a quick texture effect, use a scatter-type brush to create a textured area near the top of the image.

Save it as a PNG image type, preserving the alpha channel, in the `images` directory of webhost.

How to do it...

Create your HTML with a header element that will contain the text you want to apply your texture mask to. Then, add some text in it:

```
<h1 class="masked">I think, therefore I am</h1>
```

Then, add your CSS markup. This will include a large font size (to show off your mask texture!), a white color font, padding and alignment, and then, of course the image mask property.

 Note that each browser requires its own prefix for the property.

```
h1.masked{
    font: 140px "Arial";
    color: white;
    -webkit-mask-image: url(images/mask2.png);
    -o-mask-image: url(images/mask2.png);
    -moz-mask-image: url(images/mask2.png);
    mask-image: url(images/mask2.png);
    text-shadow: 0px 0px 10px #f0f0f0;
    width: 100%;
    padding: 12% 0 12%;
    margin:0;
    text-align: center;
}
```

The CSS effect is displayed in the following screenshot:

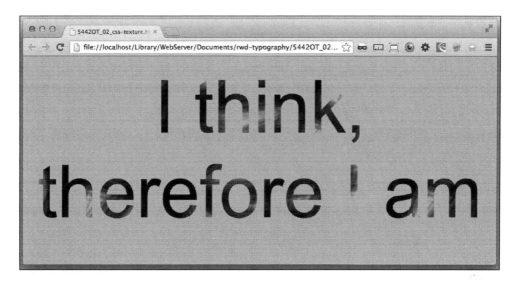

How it works...

The mask image cuts out the visible portion of the element according to the mask image's alpha. When applied over the text in the CSS, it will cut out the masked portions. This works in a very similar way to the image-editing software's alpha channel layer.

Styling alternating rows with the nth positional pseudo class

The positional-pseudo classes in CSS3 offers easy CSS solutions to problems that previously required annoyingly complicated solutions. Until very recently, to style alternating rows of a list or table, if you were fortunate enough to be able to work on a server with some sort of logic, you could at least iterate through a count in a list, or if unlucky, you had to manually numerate your rows.

Getting ready

The CSS3 solution is surprisingly simple. First, create your HTML list of values. This does not necessarily require a name-spaced class, as you might want this to be an universal style throughout your site:

```
<ul>
    <li>
        I think, therefore I am
```

```
        </li>
        <li>
            I think before I act
        </li>
        <li>
            I think I can, I think I can
        </li>
    </ul>
```

How to do it...

Add a CSS property for the list item, `<li>`, with the *n*th positional pseudo-class odd value. Give it a value of a background color and font color that is noticeably different than your default color scheme.

```
    ul{
width:100px;
    }
    li:nth-of-type(odd){
background-color:#333;
color:#f0f0f0;
    }
```

This will auto magically style the odd numbered rows of your list! The following screenshot illustrates this effect:

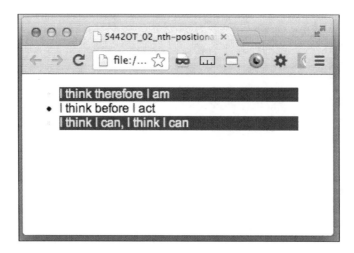

Now take a breath; that was so easy!

How it works...

According to `http://www.w3.org`, the `:nth-of-type(an+b)` pseudo-class notation represents an element that has *an+b-1* siblings with the same expanded element name before it, in the document tree for any zero or positive integer value of *n*, and has a parent element.

What does that mean? It means that as long as it has similar siblings inside the same parent element, you can either enter in a formula like *(-n+2)* for the last two rows of the siblings, or keeping it simple, even or odd, and style those rows via CSS.

Adding characters before and after pseudo elements

In what seems like a lost episode of *The Twilight Zone*, a new property of CSS gives you the ability to add pseudo markup to your content. As strange as it may sound, there are a surprising number of use cases for this sort of styling. You may want to wrap a section of your content in quotes, and not have to deal with the extra coding trouble to put quotes in your content or theme file, which of course is a sensible thing to do. Or perhaps you want to join in with the popularity of Twitter and its hash-tag and the @ markups, you can precede your content with a # or @ symbol, just by using CSS markup, as shown in the following code line:

```
#I think, therefore I am#
```

Getting ready

This requires no server-side logic or fancy footwork of any kind. All you need is to be able to launch the page in your localhost to see it in action.

How to do it...

This is accomplished with CSS only, therefore all you need to create in your HTML is a `class` or `id` property wrapped around the target content:

```
<h2 class="hashtag">I think, therefore I am</h2>
```

The CSS markup is only a bit complicated, in that the inserted symbol adheres to the margin and padding rules of the content. It uses the *n*th `class:before` and `class:after` pseudo classes. So, the CSS for `before` is `.class:before {content:"#";}`. Simply replace # with whatever symbol you want to use. And for `after`, replace `.class:before{}` with `.class:after{}`.

```
.hashtag {
    border:1px solid #ccc;
```

```
            display:block;
            width:200px;
            height:10px;
                    }
    .hashtag:before{
        content:"#";
                }
    .hashtag:after{
        content:"#";
                }
```

How it works...

The `before` and `after` pseudo elements in CSS generates content before or after the element's content. Be careful that they are not real content or elements, and cannot be used for markup or JavaScript event triggers.

Making a button with a relative font size

There are several use cases for having a responsive button font size. A good example of a use case is for mobile versions of your site. When a regular button is viewed on your iPhone, it is tiny and difficult to press. The last thing we want to do is to create a bad experience for mobile device users through our negligence of mobile devices.

Getting ready

The goal of this recipe is to use the new font measure of REM to make a responsive button font size that will grow larger when viewed on your mobile device.

REM is a new unit introduced in CSS3, it stands for Root EM, or relative to the root font size. This is different from EM, which was relative to the parent. One way to use it is to set the size of certain elements to the base size of the body font.

How to do it...

It can be used with the `@media` query to build a responsive button for your desktop and mobile devices. Here's what to do.

First, create a simple HTML page with some filler text (`http://lipsum.com`) and a `input` type of `submit`.

```
<div>
<p>Lorem ipsum dolor sit amet, consectetur adipiscing elit. Vestibulum
vehicula enim at dolor ultricies ut viverra massa rutrum. Nunc
pharetra, ipsum ut ullamcorper placerat,
```

```
</p>
    <input type="submit">
</div>
```

Next add CSS for the HTML's base font size at 62.5%, and a static font size for the paragraph, as an experimental control group:

```
html{font-size:62.5%;}
p{font-size:1.4rem;}
```

The next step is to create your @media query for the mobile device, and two different desktop window sizes. I'm adding an additional @media query for desktop screens, so if you do not have access to a mobile device you can still see the responsiveness in action.

Set up two @media queries for the desktop at 1024px and 1280px and two for mobile devices, both with max-device-width:480px, one with orientation:landscape, and other one with orientation:portrait.

```
@media screen and (min-width:1024px){ }
@media screen and (min-width:1280px){ }
@media screen and (max-device-width: 480px) and
(orientation:landscape){ }
@media screen and (max-device-width: 480px) and (orientation:portrait)
{ }
```

In your desktop @media queries, add an input element to both; and a font-size:1rem value to the min-width:1024px query, and a font-size:2rem value to the min-width:1280px query. To both queries add the properties: width:84px; and padding:2%;.

In the mobile @media queries, add the input element to both. In the orientation:landscape media query, assign the properties: font-size:2rem; and width:25%;. And in the orientation:portrait media query, assign the properties: font-size:2.4rem; and width:30%;.

```
@media screen and (min-width:1024px){
        input{
            font-size:1rem;
            width:84px;
            padding:2%;}
    }
@media screen and (min-width:1280px){
    input{
        font-size:2rem;
        width:84px;
        padding:2%;
```

```
        }
    }
    @media screen and (max-device-width: 480px) and
    (orientation:landscape){
        input{
            font-size:2rem;
            width:25%;
            padding:2%;
        }
    }
    @media screen and (max-device-width: 480px) and
    (orientation:portrait){
        input{
            font-size:2.4rem;
            width:30%;
            padding:2%;
        }
    }
}
```

Now when you view this page from a mobile device you can see how the REM size unit creates a font, sized relative to the base font. The mobile device may render the font so small it is hardly readable, and the button too small to use without fumbling. Turn the device from portrait orientation to landscape and you will see the button and its font change sizes.

Compare the mobile device button to the desktop versions. You will see the button displays unique properties per device type. And, as you drag the desktop browser window between the 1024px and 1280px sizes the button font changes also.

How it works...

The REM font size unit creates a font size relative to the base font size declared in the HTML or body elements, or if undeclared relative to the built-in base size of the font. The @media query we wrote gives a new relative size for the different devices and orientations.

Adding a shadow to your font

With CSS3 you can easily add a shadow to your text. This effect can be used to either give a special element a highlighted effect, or used throughout your body text to enhance the look of your content. In addition, you can use it to highlight links within your text to help them stand out.

Getting ready

CSS3 makes this easy, so there isn't a big setup. Open your development environment, or a Notepad program and get started. You can also go online to Packt Publishing's web page for this book and get the completed code and take a look inside.

How to do it...

First, create a paragraph element of text; recall that you can get this from our favorite filler text generator, `http://lipsum.com`. And give the text a title header:

```
<h1>I think therefore I am </h1>
<p>Lorem ipsum dolor sit amet…
</p>
```

In your paragraph, insert some links, by wrapping a couple of words in an `href` tag:

```
<h1>I think therefore I am</h1>
<p>Morbi<a href ="#">venenatis</a>Lorem ipsum dolor sit amet…
<a href ="#">scelerisque</a> Lorem ipsum dolor sit amet…</p>
```

First, let's give your paragraph text a drop shadow, this is a simple CSS3 `dropshadow` effect we can use on the text. Add the property `text-shadow` in your CSS. For Internet Explorer, add the `filter` property.

```
text-shadow: 1px 1px 2px #333333;
```

This gives your text a slight shadow that makes it pop off the page. For body text, anything more than a slight shadow will be too much. Foryour links, to make them stand out more, we can add multiple levels of text shadow. Add a shadow similar to the previous example, and then following a comma, add another shadow effect. This example adds a light blue shadow to the link text.

```
text-shadow: 0px 0px 1px blue, 1px 1px 2px #333333;
filter: dropshadow(color=blue, offx=1, offy=1);
```

Let's add an old property to give the page some new shine. Let's make your links flash on the pseudo-action hover (`:hover`):

```
p.shadowa:hover{
text-shadow: 0px 0px 8px #ffff00, 2px 2px 3px #666; filter:
dropshadow(color=#ffff00, offx=1, offy=1);
}
```

This property makes the links in the paragraph flash with a yellow glow, when you hover over them. This effect illustrated in the following screenshot:

How it works...

This recipe is a combination of shadow effects. You can combine multiple shadow effects to create realistic 3D effects for your type. The best way to learn is to experiment until you are extremely satisfied with your 3D effects.

Curving a corner with border radius

Curved corners were at one time the Holy Grail of the web design world. It was always possible, but never simple. A designer had a limited number of bad choices to employ to make an element have a curved corner.

Getting ready

This is now achieved without too much fuss with CSS3. The `border-radius` property is a simple method of creating a rounded corner on an element.

How to do it...

First create your HTML element. This works on any element that can have a border. So let's make a paragraph block of text. You can get filler text at `http://lipsum.com`.

```
<p class="rounded"> Lorem ipsum dolor sit amet...</p>
```

Next add CSS to fill out the paragraph element:

```
.rounded{
        background-color:#ccc;
        width:200px;
        margin:20px;
        padding:20px;
    }
```

Then, to round the corners, add the CSS3 property, `border-radius`. In this example, I used a curve radius of 5px.

```
border-radius: 5px;
-webkit-background-clip: padding-box;
background-clip: padding-box;
```

This property gives you simple and easy-rounded corners. This is great for a floating element on a page. But what if you wanted to round only the top corners for a menu element? Still easy.

Let's start with a simple inline list:

```
<ul class="inline">
    <li class="rounded-top"><a href="#">menu 1</a></li>
    <li class="rounded-top"><a href="#">menu 2</a></li>
    <li class="rounded-top"><a href="#">menu 3</a></li>
    <li class="rounded-top"><a href="#">menu 4</a></li>
</ul>
```

Next add the CSS to make the list inline, with padding and margins:

```
li.rounded-top{
    display:inline;
    background-color:#ccc;
    margin:3px;
    padding:8px;
}
```

The CSS in the previous example gives you rounded corners for all the corners. To have different rounded corners, specify a radius for each corner.

```
border-radius: 8px 8px 1px 1px;
```

You can achieve the same results by specifying each corner as its own CSS property:

```
border-top-left-radius:8px;
border-top-right-radius:8px;
border-bottom-right-radius:2px;
border-bottom-left-radius:2px;
```

You can take this further by adding another level of curved radius:

```
border-top-left-radius:8px 4px;
border-top-right-radius:8px 4px;
border-bottom-right-radius:2px;
border-bottom-left-radius:2px;
```

The new look is shown in the following screenshot:

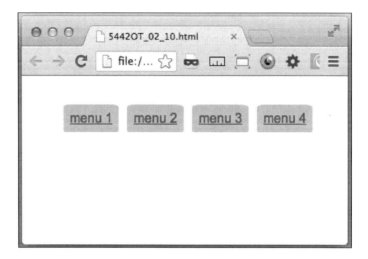

To add another level of responsiveness try replacing the curved radius entries with percentages. Go back to the first example in this recipe and change the CSS to have a percent radius curve:

```
border-radius: 1%;
```

How it works...

The `border-radius` property provides a simple rendering of a curve on an element. This property takes four values, but can be written in the shorthand format with only one curve radius.

3
Responsive Layout

In this chapter, you will learn about:

- ▶ Responsive layout with the min-width and max-width properties
- ▶ Controlling your layout with relative padding
- ▶ Adding a media query to your CSS
- ▶ Creating a responsive width layout with media queries
- ▶ Changing image sizes with media queries
- ▶ Hiding an element with media queries
- ▶ Making a smoothly transitioning responsive layout

Introduction

This chapter has some challenging recipes. Responsive layouts often present some difficult challenges that can push you to create a great solution. With responsive design methods you can do much more, and do it more efficiently. Responsive layouts have introduced a whole new area of challenges to web development and a new dimension of excitement.

Responsive layout with the min-width and max-width properties

Many responsive layout techniques can be quite complex and overwhelming, but in this recipe you will see a fairly simple layout using the `min-width` and `max-width` properties applied to three floating elements. With this very simple responsive layout feature of CSS, you are ready to display your site on mobile devices and desktop screens of various sizes.

Getting ready

Floating elements that collapse from multiple columns into one column on a small viewport is not a new trick. This has been around for years as a standard property of CSS1, however, there was never any reason to consider it useful until the mobile devices became common. So let's combine this old, stale property with some other fresh CSS properties to make a responsive layout.

How to do it...

Create a simple HTML page enclosed in an `article` element, containing a `h1` header and three elements. The first element will contain an image and the second and third will contain filler text. Assign to all of the inner elements a class of `float` and respectively `one`, `two`, and `three` as their IDs:

```
<article>
      <h1>Responsive Layout with min and max width</h1>

      <div class="one float">
         <img src="images/robot.png">
      </div>

      <div class ="two float">Pellentesqueeleifendfacilisisodio ac
      ullamcorper. Nullamutenimutmassatinciduntluctus...
      </div>

      <div class="three float">Pellentesqueeleifendfacilisisodio ac
      ullamcorper. Nullamutenimutmassatinciduntluctus. Utnullalibero, …
      </div>
</article>
```

Next, create your style for the `.article` element and assign the properties: `width: 100%;`, `max-width: 1280px;`, and auto side margins. Then, center the h1 title. Assign the `img` element the `width: 100%` and `height: auto;` properties to make it responsive to its parent element. For the floating element containing the `img` element, give it a `min-width` value of `500px`. You could also give each floating element a different background color to make them more discernible, but this is not vital to the layout. To all the floating elements in the `.float` class, add a `max-width: 350px` property, left float, and for clean looks, justify the text.

```
<style>
article{
      width: 100%;
```

```
        max-width: 1280px;
        margin: 0 auto;
    }
    h1 {text-align:center;}
    img {
        width: 100%;
        height: auto;
    }
    .one {
        background-color: #333;
        min-width: 500px;
    }
    .two {background-color:#666}
    .three {background-color:#ccc}
    .float {
        max-width: 350px;
        float: left;
        text-align: justify;
    }
    }
        </style>
```

Once everything is put together and you have the HTML document open in your browser, you will see how the layout smoothly goes from a three-column layout to a two-column layout, and then finally to a single-column layout, as shown in the following screenshot:

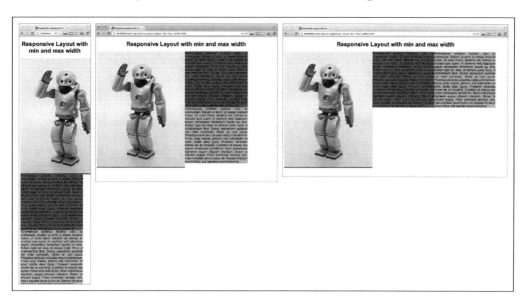

How it works...

The `max-width` property of the columns allows them to have a fluid but a maximum width. This gives you more flexibility in the layout of the columns than you would have with a static width. The image column utilizes the `min-width` property so it can respond to parent element width's changes by growing and shrinking. Finally, the whole layout can smoothly break down from three columns to one column by using the `float` property; once there is not enough room for the elements to float side by side, the last element drops to a new row.

Controlling your layout with relative padding

Let's put together a simple layout for a blog with comments and comment replies. This is possible using only relative padding for the layout. You say, "That's crazy! How can you control a page layout with nothing but padding?" Let's find out.

Getting ready

Of course, a blog is much more dynamic than a static HTML page, so this would be a good part of a comments template section for your favorite blogging software. That being said, this recipe is remarkably easy, and yet effective. So, go get yourself some Ipsum filler text and get ready to troll yourself.

How to do it...

The first step is to create a very simple blog style page with comments embedded in the `div` element. In your HTML body, create the element that will hold everything, the `.content` div. Give it a `h1` title, a paragraph of Ipsum filler text, and follow it with a `.comments` element. Inside the `.comments` element you will build your embedded comments layout.

```
<div class="content">
        <header>Control your layout with relative padding</header>
        <p>
Pellent esque eleifend facilis isodio ac ullam corper. Null amuten
imut massat incident luctus. Utnull alibero, el eifend vel ultrices
at, volut patquis quam...</p>
        <div class="comments">
            <h2>Comments</h2> No 2 x h1
        </div>
</div>
```

Under the `.comments` title, you will add your first comment. And next, inside that comment, immediately after the closing paragraph tag add a comment to that comment:

```
<aside>
    <h1>Comments</h1>
    <div class="comment">
        <p>
Pellent esque eleifend facilis isodio ac ullam corper. Null amuten
imut massat incident luctus. Utnull alibero, et...
        </p>
        <div class="comment">
            <p>
Pellent esque eleifend facilis isodio ac ullam corper. Null amuteni
mut massat incident luctus. Ut null alibero, el eifend vel ultrices
at, volut patquis quam...
            </p>
        </div>
    </div>
</aside>
```

Continuing from there, you can insert more comments the same way to a comment on the parent comment, or add a comment outside of the parent `div` element to make the comment to the parents' parent, all the way up to the original blog post:

```
<aside>
    <h1>Comments</h1>
      <div class="comment">
        <p>
            Pellent esque el eifend facilis isodio ac ullam corper..
        </p>

      <div class="comment">
        <p>
            Null amuten imut massat incident luctus....
        </p>

      <div class="comment">
        <p>
            Ut null alibero, el eifend velul trices at, volut pat quis
quam...
        </p>
      </div>
```

```
        </div>
      </div>
    <div class="comment">
        <p>
            Null ameget dui eros, et semper justo. Nun cut condi mentum
felis...
        </p>
      </div>
    </div>

  </aside>
```

Eventually, you can have many comments and a good looking working layout built simply with only relative padding.

The CSS to make this work is surprisingly easy. Simply add the classes: `.content`, `.comments`, and `.comment`. In the `content` class add some side padding, and in the `comment` add heavier padding to the left.

```
.content {padding:0 5% 0 5%;}
aside {padding:0 10% 0 20%}
.comment {padding:0 0 0 10%}
```

This is illustrated in the following screenshot:

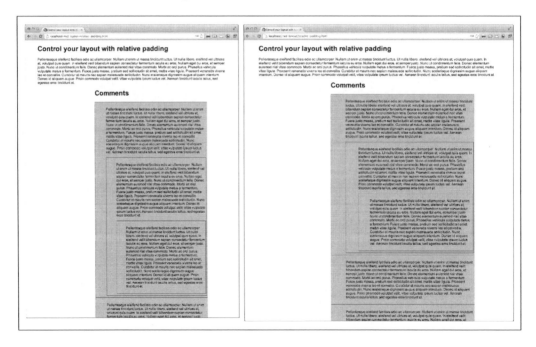

How it works...

The relative padding attribute responds to page width changes by adjusting its own width.

Adding a media query to your CSS

In this recipe, we will explore the awesome power of the media query by rendering a simple web page with every permutation and device available in the universe. Okay, I'm exaggerating a little, I admit. But we will create a simple web page that will respond to several browser window sizes, devices, and other possible presentation methods.

Getting ready

Solely for the purpose of this recipe, go out and purchase one of each of the devices and variations described here. You'll need a new high definition TV, a smart phone, a not-so-smart phone, and at least one printer. No way? Okay, but I'm just trying to help you and the economy. That being said, of course it will be impossible to truly test every media query, but do what you can. There are a surprising number of possibilities. But in most real-life scenarios, you are unlikely to need or care to use most of these. We will at least try to cover the most commonly used media queries.

I will skip over those that I think are unnecessary to you. You can easily access information about these if you find yourself in a project with requirements to create presentations for one of these obscure devices. You never know! The WC3 has all of the detailed information and descriptions of these if you need them at `http://www.w3.org/TR/css3-mediaqueries/`. I will exclude the examples and just for your reference include numerous devices with specific color limitations, including monochrome, print, TV, and handheld. The media queries you will need most likely are `screen` and `print`.

How to do it...

Create a simple HTML page with a `h1` title, and an element wrapping around an image, and a paragraph of text. Get some Ipsum filler text if you don't have any text lying around. It will look just like the following:

```
<body>
    <h1>Add Media Query to your CSS</h1>
        <div class="wrap">
            <img src="images/robot.png"/>
Pellent esque el eifend facilisis odio ac ullam corper. Nullam ut enim
ut massa tincidunt luctus...
        </div>
</body>
```

Next create a series of media queries. In the following list, I will give a brief explanation of what each does:

```
@media print{...}
```

This is applied to the web page when it's printed. You can test this by selecting **File | Print** and then view the print preview. This is useful for web pages where users will be printing it as a document to read. You can take advantage of this and change or remove the formatting to make this version as simple as possible.

```
@media (orientation: portrait){...}
```

This is generally applied on any device that shows the document in portrait mode. You can use it for mobile devices to change the look for different orientations. Be cautious because this also will be applied to desktop screens unless you specify it to smaller screens or devices only. The media query orientation's other possible value is landscape.

```
@media (height:500px){...}
```

The `height` and `width` media query allows you to specify style for specific screen dimensions.

```
@media (device-width:500px){...}
```

This media query will apply a style to any page, regardless of browser's window size, that is viewed on a device of the specified dimensions.

```
@media screen and (device-aspect-ratio: 16/9) {...}
```

This media query can be used to define styles for screens (not print) with a view window of the `16/9` ratio.

```
@media tv {...}
```

This aspect ratio would apply only to a device using a television to view.

```
@media screen and (max-width:960px){...}
@media screen and (min-width:961px) and (max-width:1280px){...}
@media screen and (min-width:1281px) and (max-width:1336px){...}
@media screen and (min-width:1336px){...}
```

The `min-width` and `max-width` media queries are the most useful one. Here, you can define a responsive style for any window size including the small-screen mobile devices. I typically start by defining the smallest—or mobiles—viewports breakpoint, and define their styles, and then create breakpoint ranges for the most popular screen sizes, ending with a `min-width` media query to apply to the largest screen sizes.

Once you have created the media queries that you think are useful for your current project, add styles to the media queries with different values:

```
@media tv {
      body {color: blue;}
      h1 {
            font-weight: bold;
            font-size: 140%;
      }
      img {
            float: left;
            width: 20%;
            border: 2px solid #ccc;
            padding: 2%;
            margin: 2%;
      }
      p {
            width: 62%;
            float: right;
            font-size: 110%;
            padding: 2%;
      }
}
@media screen and (max-width: 960px) {
      body {color: #000;}
      h1 {
            font-weight: bold;
            font-size: 120%;
      }
      img {
            float: right;
            width: 20%;
            border: 2px solid #ccc;
            padding: 1%;
            margin: 1%;
      }
      P {
            width: 80%;
            float: left;
            font-size: 60%;
      }
}
```

```
@media screen and (min-width:961px) and (max-width:1280px) {
    body {color: #000000;}
    h1 {
        font-weight: bold;
        font-size: 120%;
    }
    img {
        float: right;
        width: 20%;
        border: 2px solid #ccc;
        padding: 1%;
        margin: 1%;
    }
    P {
        width: 76%;
        float: left;
        font-size: 60%;
    }
}
@media screen and (min-width: 1281px) {
    body {color: #000000;}
    h1 {
        font-weight: bold;
        font-size: 120%;
    }
    img {
        float: right;
        width: 20%;
        border: 2px solid #ccc;
        padding: 1%;
        margin: 1%;
    }
    P {
        width: 70%;
        float: left;
        font-size: 100%;
    }
}
```

The final version of the page is displayed in the following screenshot:

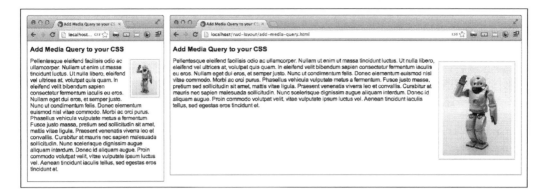

How it works...

Apply these styles and you will find that a different style is applied to different devices. You can combine a number of these in a clever way to create magic responsiveness in your site.

Creating a responsive width layout with media queries

In this recipe we will make a simple responsive width layout that adjusts itself to various screen widths. This layout would be a good starter template for a personal blog or news magazine, where you would want your readers to comment on your content and on each other's comments. It may even be a great theme starter to attract trolls to a flame war. This paragraph just sounds silly, sorry!

Getting ready

This template will work great in a dynamic CMS or blog software, but might not make much sense as a plain HTML page. But most themes work in the same as HTML as far as presentation goes. In most cases, you would simply replace the text and static navigation with template tags. This recipe will need some filler text to demonstrate. If you do not already have some text to work with, go to our old standby Ipsum generator to get some filler text.

How to do it...

To begin, create a simple web page, and in the `style` element create your media queries. You can always link to an external stylesheet, but for the sake of simplicity, this and most of the recipes contain the CSS in the `<style>...</style>` section of your header. Include these standard breakpoints at screen sizes: `960`, `1024`, and `1280`.

```
<style>
@media screen and (max-width: 960px) {...}
@media screen and (min-width: 961px) and (max-width: 1024px) {...}
@media screen and (min-width: 1025px) and (max-width: 1280px) {...}
@media screen and (min-width: 1281px) {...}
</style>
```

The first media query affects all viewports narrower than `960px`. The second from `961px` to `1024px`, the third from `1025px` to `1280px`, and the last affects, all screen sizes larger than `1281px`. Within each media query, you will write a CSS for a different layout. There will be some layout CSS outside of the media query along with your style presentation, but most of them will be defined in the media queries.

The next step is to create your HTML layout. The basic structure starts with these basic `div` elements—`nav`, `content`, and `comments`:

```
<body>
    <nav></nav>
    <div class="content"></div>
    <aside class="comments"></aside>
</body>
```

Next add some filler content to your page. This will aid in the demonstration of the layout.

In the `nav` element, add an unordered list with sample menu links. This will serve as a responsive menu. At the pages' narrowest width, the menu will display vertically. In widths ranging from 961px to 1280px, the menu is displayed inline horizontally on top. For larger widths, we want the menu to return to a vertical display and return to the left-hand side.

In the first two media queries, the `content` and `comments` elements will float left, but with different width ratios. In `960px`, these elements should have a width of `90%`. In the larger widths, set the `content` and `comments` elements at `60%` and `20%`, respectively.

```
@media screen and (max-width: 960px) {
        .content {width: 90%;}
        .comments {width: 90%;}
    }
```

```
@media screen and (min-width: 961px) and (max-width: 1280px) {
      .nav ul li {display: inline-block;}
      .content {width: 60%;}
      .comments {width: 20%;}
@media screen and (min-width: 1281px) {
      .content {width: 60%;}
      .comments {width: 20%;}
}
```

To make the menu slide back to the left on the large screens, we will use positioning to create a three column layout. In the `min-width:1281px` media query, add the `.nav` element and styles for absolute positioning and width:

```
.nav{
      position: absolute;
      top: 20px;
      left: 0px;
      width:144px;
}
```

That's almost all the steps necessary to build a responsive layout. To tidy things up, let's add some padding to the layouts. Add the `.nav`, `.content`, and `.comments` elements to the other media queries, and then add padding to those. Refer to the following CSS. The `min-width:1281px` media query will not have a padding for the `.nav` element, and the padding for the `.content` and `.comments` elements are reduced to allow for the vertical menu.

```
@media screen and (max-width: 960px){
      .nav {padding: 1% 5%;}
      .content,.comments {padding: 1% 5%;}
      .content {width: 90%;}
}
@media screen and (min-width: 961px) and (max-width: 1280px){
      .nav {padding: 1% 5%;}
      .nav ul li {display: inline;}
      .content,.comments {padding: 1% 5%;}
      .content {width: 60%;}
}
@media screen and (min-width: 1281px){
      .nav {
            position: absolute;
            top: 20px;
            left: 0px;
            width: 144px;
      }
```

```
.content,.comments {padding: 1% 1% 1% 0;}
.content{
    width: 60%;
    margin-left: 144px;
}
}
```

You can also style the inline menu however you want. For now let's simply add some margins to the `li` elements. Add this element and styles outside of the media queries, `.nav ul li{margin: 2px 10px;}`.

Finally, on to the content and comments, paste your filler text inside the `.content` element. I also added the header and paragraph tags inside. We will do something similar for the comments.

Remember that we want to allow for embedded comments, or people to comment on comments. There will be a possible inherited hierarchy of comments, and we still need this to look good in all browser sizes, so we should add some padding. Adding a static padding to the `.comment` element will not look good in all browser sizes. Instead, add a relative padding to each media query's `.comments` element, so that they take less space as the browser window gets smaller: `90%` for the `max-width:960px` media query and `20%` for all larger sizes. Add outside of the media queries, `padding-left: 8%` to the `.comment` element, and float the `.content` and `.comments` elements to the `left`. You can also `text-align:justify` them to make the text look like a block.

```
@media screen and (max-width: 960px) {
    .nav {padding: 1% 5%;}
    .content,.comments {padding: 1% 5%;}
    .content {width: 90%;}
    .comments {width: 90%;}
}
@media screen and (min-width: 961px) and (max-width: 1280px) {
    .nav {padding: 1% 5%;}
    .nav ul li {display: inline;}
    .content,.comments {padding: 1% 5%;}
    .content {width: 60%;}
    .comments {width: 20%;}
}
@media screen and (min-width: 1281px) {
    .nav {
        position: absolute;
        top: 20px;
        left: 0;
        width: 144px;
    }
```

```
.content,.comments {padding:1% 1% 1% 0}
.content {
    width: 60%;
    margin-left: 144px;
}
.comments { width: 20%;}
}
.content,.comments {
    float: left;
    text-align: justify;
}
.nav ul li {margin: 2px 10px;}
.comment {padding-left: 8%;}
```

This CSS will make the padding on comments and embedded comments adjust to the changes in the browser window sizes. As a result, the comments section of your page will show the comment parent-and-child hierarchy, as well as a consistent and workable layout for each browser window size. You can see the code in action demonstrated in the following screenshot:

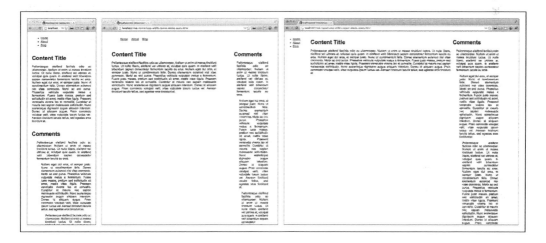

How it works...

In this responsive layout we used a few different techniques. First, the media query offers us limited but useful logic to deploy different layout techniques for different browser window sizes. Second, the fluid and floating elements with size ratios adjust with ease to the new layouts. And last but not least, fluid's percent-based padding gives a consistent ratio of padding to the screen size and layout.

Changing image sizes with media queries

In this recipe, you will learn how to resize an image with a CSS media query. This can be useful in a number of situations, especially those where you want to download only one image and use it in different size versions in your responsive layout.

Getting ready

This is a good method for size variation that can be handled on the client side, but be careful not to abuse this method by causing the client to download a really large image file and do heavy resizing in their browser. There are better ways to do that, which were discussed in *Chapter 1, Responsive Elements and Media.*

How to do it...

I recommend putting together a small HTML page with a h1 title, the `wrap` element, and inside `wrap`, an image and a paragraph of text. You really don't need all of this extra stuff to make an image size change in an image query, however, it will help you demonstrate the use of changing an image size in the media query.

Next, create your media queries for the most frequent browser window size breakpoints: `960px`, `1024px`, `1280px`, `1366px`, `1440px`, and last but not least `1680px`. In each of these media queries, add your styles for the elements. In my example, I created media queries at `960px` and `1280px`:

```
@media screen and (max-width: 960px){
    .wrap {padding:0 5%; width: 90%;}
    .wrap img {
        width: 90%;
        height: auto;
        padding:5%;
    }
    .wrap p {
        width: 90%;
        padding: 5%;
        text-align: justify;
    }
}
@media screen and (min-width: 961px) and (max-width: 1280px) {
    .wrap {
        padding: 0 5%;
        width: 90%;
    }
    .wrap img {
        width: 50%;
```

```
        height: auto;
        max-width: 600px;
        float: right;
        }
    .wrap p {
        width: 50%;
        text-align: justify;
        float: left;
    }
}
@media screen and (min-width:1281px) {
    .wrap {
        padding: 0 5%;
        width: 90%;
    }
    .wrap img {
        width: 40%;
        height: auto;
        max-width: 500px;
        float: left;
    }
    .wrap p {
        width: 60%;
        text-align: justify;
        float: right;
    }
}
```

Now as you resize your page you can see how the image resizes as the browser resizes through the various media queries. This is illustrated in the following screenshot:

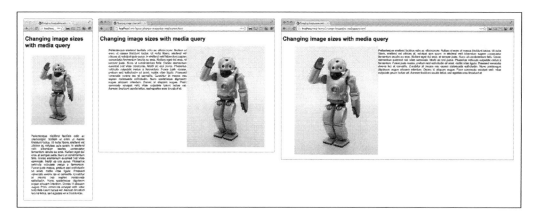

How it works...

The different media queries, when called by the browser, present different sizes for the element's `width` and `height` property. This allows you to optimize your image size for different devices. Use your judgment, and if the original image is too large, look into some server-side resizing as an alternate method.

Hiding an element with media queries

This recipe will show you some very useful tricks with media queries to make elements disappear off the screen, depending on the browser window's size. There are a few different methods of hiding an element on the screen, I will go through three of them in this recipe.

Getting ready

This method can have a number of use cases. One very helpful case is using it to switch out menus on the fly when scaling a page down to a smaller device. You could also use this to change the way your content areas or aside contents are displayed. The possibilities are unlimited when you get creative with the methods.

How to do it...

Set up a simple page for demonstration. In my example, I wrote up a page with a `h1` header, an image, and then two elements with text inside them. Next, add some style to those elements. I added a different background color and width properties to each element, mostly, so that I could keep them apart when they disappeared.

And then add your media queries at a breakpoint. In the example, I'll add a breakpoint at `960px`. And inside the media queries, we're going to take a look at some different methods of getting the element to disappear.

In your first media query, `max-width: 960px`, add the position: absolute and left: 5000px properties for the `img` element; This style will move the element far enough to the left of the screen that it has for all practical purposes, disappeared. Add to that media query a `display: none` style to the `.bar` element. This leaves the element where it is, but renders it invisible. Both of these elements are are effectively gone from the page, leaving only the title and `.foo` elements.

In the second media query, you will try a different way to remove an element from the screen. First, add the `.foo` element to the media query and give it a left margin of `5000px`. That removes it from the screen, however, the next element clears its vertical space and leaves an obvious white space where the element was. Then, float the element to the left and the white space will disappear. This is illustrated in the following code snippet:

```
.foo {
    background-color: #ccc;
    width: 300px;
}
.bar {
    background-color: blue;
    width: 600px;
    color: white;
}
@media screen and (max-width: 960px) {
    img {
        position: absolute;
        left: 5000px;
    }
    .bar {display: none;}
}
@media screen and (min-width: 961px) {
    .foo {
        float: left;
        margin-left: -5000px;
    }
}
```

Congratulations! Open the project in your browser and see if it looks like the following screenshot:

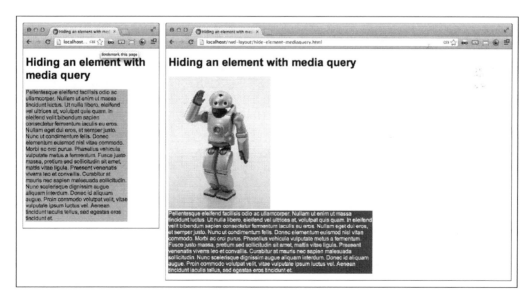

How it works...

Both the absolute position and float do not have a height property, so once applied to an element, they will not occupy any vertical space. This can be an especially useful trick to move elements around on your page. It can also cause some problems when you use floating elements for layout. This behavior can be fixed by inserting a break with a `clear:both` property after the element.

Making a smoothly transitioning responsive layout

In this recipe I will guide you through the creation of a multi-zoned and responsive front page. This one will have a number of elements that are responsive in different ways; giving a rich user experience that delivers an impressive layout. I developed this for a startup I was working on and found that I liked it so much that I continued to develop it further to share with you in this recipe.

Getting ready

This recipe will be a good template for a homepage to a content-heavy site. If you have been building content for a while, this will be perfect for the landing page, and can be modified for a single-item content page easily. If you are just getting started with your site, you can go get some generated text at `http://lipsum.com` like I did for this recipe.

How to do it...

This site breaks down into three HTML elements or a footer, and two elements that sometimes are vertical and sometimes are left and right floats—depending on the screen width. These elements themselves are also divided into smaller elements. So, get started and create a basic page with a top-wrap element, a middle-wrap element, and a footer:

```
<body>
  <header>...</header>
  <div class="content" role="main">...</div>
  <footer>...</footer>
</body>
```

Next, we start the CSS for these items. Add some basic CSS and the following media queries:

```
body{
    margin: 0;
    padding: 0;
}
```

```
footer {width: 100%;}
.clear {clear: both;}
@media screen and (max-width: 1280px) {
     header, .content {width: 100%;}
}
@media screen and (min-width: 1281px) {
     header {
          float: left;
          width: 60%;
     }
     .content {
          float: right;
          width: 40%;
     }
}
```

In this basic layout, the `header` and `.content` rows both occupy `100%` of the page width, while the page is under `1280px`. When the page is larger, they occupy the respective `60%`/`40%` split and the float `left` and `right`.

Next let's build the menus. This menu will employ a responsive trick of using a media query to hide and show two different menus. Essentially, we will build two different menus, and then use CSS to display the optimized one for each screen. The smallest version will use a multi-select drop-down menu, while the larger menu contains two inline lists. Here's what the HTML looks like inside the top-wrap element:

```
<header>
    <nav>
        <div class="menu small-menu">
            <img src="images/robot-low.png">
            <form>
                <select name="URL" onchange='window.location.
href=this.form.URL.options[this.form.URL.selectedIndex].value'>
                <option value="blog.html">Page 1</option>
                <option value="home.html">Home Page</option>
                <option value="tutorials.html">Tutorials</option>
                </select>
            </form>
        </div>

        <div class="menu large-menu">
            <div class="top-menu">
                <nav>
                  <ul>
```

```
                    <li><a href="login.html">Log In</a></li>
                    <li><a href="account.html">My Account</a></li>
                </ul>
            </nav>
        </div>
        <div class="bottom-menu"> these should be classes so they can
be reused. Plus the names are too specific.
            <nav>
                <a href="#" class="logo">
                    <img src="images/robot-low.png">
                </a>
                <ul>
                    <li><a href="blog.html">Page 1</a></li>
                    <li><a href="home.html">Home Page</a></li>
                    <li><a href="tutorials.html">Tutorials</a></li>
                    <li> <a href="news.html">News</a> </li>
                </ul>
            </nav>
        </div>
    </div>
    </nav>
</header>
```

Add the following CSS for the header elements:

```
nav .small-menu img{
    width:9%;
    height:auto;
    float:left;
    padding:0 2%;
}
nav .small-menu select {
    margin: 3%;
    width: 80%;
}
```

This will display two different versions of the menu until we add to our media queries.
Add media queries to switch between displaying the drop-down menu on small browser
windows and the larger inline list menu on larger browser window sizes. Use the display
property to show and hide the menus.

```
@media screen and (max-width: 600px) {
    nav .small-menu {display: inline;}
    nav .large-menu {display: none;}
}
```

```
@media screen and (min-width: 601px) {
    nav .small-menu {display: none;}
    nav .large-menu {display: inline;}
}
```

Under the menus, before the closing `</header>` tag create a space for a large high-quality photo to display on the site. And to prevent it from becoming a wasted space let's put a search box right in the middle of it. We can actually make this search form stick closely to the center of the picture and responsively adjust to screen size changes. This is illustrated in the following simple code:

```
<div class="img-search">classes
    <div class="search">
        <form>
            <input type="text" placeholder="Find a Robot">
            <input value="Search" class="search-input" type="submit">
        </form>
    </div>
    <img class="main-img" src='images/robot-wide.png'>
</div>
```

And of course the magic is in the CSS. Let's use some tricks to make the search form hover in the same spot. First give the outer `div` element a width of `100%`, then the `search` element will get an absolute position and few different properties under different media queries. This combination will keep the search form floating above the middle of the `img` area. Keep in mind that we are adding new CSS to the media queries. The following CSS code reflects only the additions, not what was already there. It gets rather long if I show the entire CSS expanding each time. At the end, I will include the entire CSS as it should be in its final state.

```
.img-search {width: 100%;}
.search {position: absolute; }
.top-menu {
    height: 33px;
    background-color: #ccc;
}
.logo img {height: 87px; float: left;}
.top-menu nav li {display: inline-block;}
.large-menu ul {margin: 0 5px;}
.large-menu li {display: inline;}

@media screen and (max-width: 600px) {
    .search {
        margin-top: 87px;
        left: 22%;}
}
```

```
@media screen and (min-width: 601px) and (max-width: 1280px) {
    .search {
        margin-top: 144px;
        left: 40%;
    }
}
@media screen and (min-width: 1281px) {
    .search {
        margin-top: 144px;
        left: 22%;
    }
}
```

The `.img-search` image element will receive a dynamic width of `100%`, and auto height. And that's it for the large image search field.

Give the next element, `.flip-tab`, a width of `100%`, and any height or other properties you want. You won't have to worry about this again:

```
<div class="flip-tab"><h3>Look Down Here</h3></div>
```

```
.flip-tab {width: 100%; height: 54px; text-align: center;}
```

The next element, `.teasers`, will get a `max-width: 1280px` property so it will auto-magically be at `100%` width of its parent element, `top-wrap`, limited to `1280px`. This element is simply a container for the three left-floating `.teaser` elements. These `.teaser` elements will have two different property sets under different media queries for a `600px` breakpoint.

```
<div class="teasers">
    <div class="teaser teaser1">
        <h3>The First Law of Robotics</h3>
            <p>
                Lorem ipsum dolor sit amet,..
            </p>
    </div>
    <div class="teaser teaser2">
        <h3>The First Law of Robotics</h3>
            <p>
                Lorem ipsum dolor sit amet,..
            </p>
    </div>
    <div class="teaser teaser3">
        <h3>The First Law of Robotics</h3>
            <p>
```

```
                    Lorem ipsum dolor sit amet,..
              </p>
       </div>
</div>
.teasers {max-width: 1280px;}
.teaser {float: left;}
@media screen and (max-width: 600px) {
      .teaser {width: 100%;}
}
@media screen and (min-width: 601px) {
      .teaser {
           width: 32%;
           min-width: 144px;
      }
}
```

That concludes everything you will be doing in the header element. Up next is the content element, which wraps the content that will float in the right-hand side columns. What's inside this element is nothing more than a two-column float split at a 60/40 ratio, or if the parent element is narrow, each is 100% wide. The content element will have two different property sets under media queries with a breakpoint at 1280px. These elements have some limited sample content. You can add much more once you deploy the layout:

```
<div class="content" role="main">
      <div class="contact-us">

            <div class="form-wrap">
                  <legend>Find a Robot</legend>

                  <form>
                        <input type="text" placeholder="Robot Search">
                        <input value="Search" class="search-input"
type="submit">
                  </form>
            </div>
                  <h4>Search or Like Us Locally</h4>
            <ul class="local-like">                  <li><a
href="/search/SanFranciso">San Francisco</a><a href="/like/
SanFrancisco">Like</a></li>
                  <li><a href="/search/LosAngeles">Los Angeles</a><a
href="/like/LosAngeles">Like</a></li>
                  <li><a href="/search/Austin">Austin</a><a href="/like/
Austin">Like</a></li>
```

```
            <li><a href="/search/Houston">Houston</a><a href="/like/
Houston">Like</a></li>            </ul>
    </div>
    <divclass="cities"> really?
        <p>Loremipsumdolor sitamet, consecteturadipiscingelit.
Nunc non felisutmetusvestibulumcondimentumuteueros.Nam id ipsumnibh.
Praesent sit ametvelit...
        </p>
    </div>

</div>
```

This CSS is more complicated, but remember, you can access this entire work online. As you can see, the elements do zig and zag around a bit, but each breakpoint will have an optimized display.

```
.contact-us {float: left;}
.cities {float: left;}
@media screen and (max-width: 600px) {
    .contact-us {width: 100%;}
    .cities {width: 100%;}
}
@media screen and (min-width: 601px) and (max-width: 1280px) {
    .contact-us {width: 40%;}
    .cities {width: 60%;}
}
@media screen and (min-width: 1281px) and (max-width: 1366px) {
    .contact-us {width: 100%;}
    .cities {width: 100%;}
}
@media screen and (min-width: 1367px) {
    .contact-us {width: 40%;}
    .cities {width: 60%;}
}
```

Finally, the footer! (The end of the page!) The footer breaks down into a 100% wide outer <footer>, and then a footer-wrap wrap with a 100% width, max-width of 1280px, dynamic side margins, and inline-block display. Inside are three elements that always have the property display:inline-block. When the display is small, these elements are each 100% wide, otherwise they are 33% wide, left-floating, with a minimum width of 144px:

```
<footer>
    <div class="footer-wrap">
        <div class="footer-1 footer-third">
            <ul>
```

```
            <li><span class=""><a href="#">FaceBook</a></span></li>
            <li><span class=""><a href="#">Google +</a></span></li>
            <li><span class=""><a href="#">Twitter</a></span></li>
            </ul>
        </div>
        <div class="footer-2 footer-third">
            <ul>
                <li><span class=""><a href="#">Link1</a></span></li>
                <li><span class=""><a href="#">Privacy Policy</a></
                span></li>
                <li><span class=""><a href="#">Terms of Use</a></
                span></li>
            </ul>
        </div>
        <div class="footer-3 footer-third">
            <ul>
                <li><span class=""><a href="#">Link1</a></span></li>
                <li><span class=""><a href="#">Link2</a></span></li>
                <li><span class=""><a href="#">Link3</a></span></li>
            </ul>
        </div>
    </div>
</footer>

.footer-wrap{
    width: 100%;
    max-width: 1280px;
    margin :0 10%;
    display: inline-block;
}
.footer-third {display: inline-block;}

@media screen and (max-width: 600px) {
    .footer-third {width :100%;}
}
@media screen and (min-width: 601px{
    .footer-third {
        float: left;
        width: 33%;
            min-width: 144px;
    }
}
```

As I promised previously, here is the full CSS code:

```css
body{margin:0;padding:0;}
.img-search {width: 100%}
.search {position:absolute;}
nav .small-menu img{width:9%;height:auto;float:left;padding:0 2%;}
nav .small-menu select {margin: 3%; width: 80%;}
.main-img {width: 100%; height: auto;}
.top-menu {height: 33px; background-color: #ccc;}
.top-menu nav li {display: inline-block;}
.logo img {height: 87px; float: left;}
.large-menu ul {margin: 0 5px;}
.large-menu li {display: inline;}

.flip-tab {width: 100%; height: 54px; text-align: center;}
.teasers {max-width: 1280px;}
.teaser {float:left;}
.contact-us {float:left;}
.cities {float:left;}

footer {width:100%}
.footer-wrap {width: 100%; max-width: 1280px; margin: 0 10%; display:
inline-block;}
.footer-third {display:inline-block;}


@media screen and (max-width: 600px) {
 nav .small-menu {display: inline}
 nav .large-menu {display: none}
 .search {margin-top: 87px; left: 22%;}
 .teaser {width: 100%}
 .contact-us {width: 100%;}
 .cities {width: 100%}
 .footer-third {width: 100%}
}
@media screen and (min-width: 601px) and (max-width: 1280px){
      .search {margin-top: 144px; left: 40%}
      .contact-us {width: 40%;}
      .cities {width: 60%}
}
```

```
@media screen and (min-width: 601px) {
 nav .small-menu{display: none}
 nav .large-menu{display: inline}
 .teaser {width: 32%; min-width: 144px;}
 .footer-third {float: left; width: 33%; min-width: 144px;}
}
@media screen and (max-width: 1280px) {
 header, .content {width: 100%;}
}
@media screen and (min-width: 1281px) {
 header {float: left; width: 60%;}
 .content {float: right; width: 40%;}
 .search {margin-top: 144px; left:22%;}
}
@media screen and (min-width: 1281px) and (max-width: 1366px){
 .contact-us {width: 100%}
 .cities {width:100%}
 }
@media screen and (min-width: 1367px) {
.contact-us {width: 40%}
.cities {width: 60%}
}
```

This one was long and difficult; thanks for hanging in there! The effect is illustrated in the following screenshot, compare this with your output:

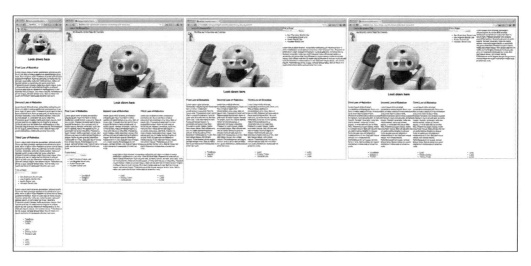

How it works...

These CSS and media queries, when combined together, make a responsive footer that can stay centered through all the screen sizes, and collapse down for small mobile-sized browser windows.

Responsive layout is an exciting new area of web development methodology. The responsive methodology allows the designer and developer to create for multiple devices, especially mobile devices, without the expense of developing native apps. Very soon, if not already, you can expect many companies to want to take a responsive approach to their site redesigns.

There's more...

You created a very simple method of responsive almost completely using CSS. I would challenge you to take this one step further by eliminating the dual menus in the `nav` element. Look in the *Adding JavaScript for mobile browsers only* recipe, in *Chapter 5, Making Mobile-first Web Applications*, to add a jQuery method to replace the large menus with the `<select>` element in mobile browsers. This will prevent any potential search engine penalty from having duplicate content in the menus.

First, cut out the `smallMenu` div element and its children, and paste it somewhere in the header, or top of the body, inside a `<script>` `</script>` element as a variable, `smallMenu`.

```
var smallMenu = '<div class="menu small-menu">...</div>'
```

Next write the script that will be called to remove the `large-menu` div element and append to the `nav` element the `smallMenu` variable.

```
$(document).ready(function() {
    $('.large-menu').remove();
    $('nav').append(smallMenu);
});
```

Now, when the page loads on a mobile device, the script will replace the navigation with a scaled-down mobile version, and you will not lose any sleep over your SEO!

4

Using Responsive Frameworks

In this chapter, you will learn about:

- ▸ Using the Fluid 960 grid layout
- ▸ Using the Blueprint grid layout
- ▸ Fluid layout using the rule of thirds
- ▸ Trying Gumby, a responsive 960 grid
- ▸ The Bootstrap framework makes responsive layouts easy

Introduction

The **layout** frameworks have become increasingly useful and widespread in layout design and development. Many web developers have found that by adapting their designs to a framework, they can speed up their production dramatically.

There are a number of good frameworks out there, which at first glance may seem like too much effort to spin up, otherwise you will have to sacrifice too much of your design to adapt to someone else's methodology. At least, that's what I thought at first. In practice, what I found was that learning and using frameworks allowed me to focus more on the parts of the project I enjoyed, and helped me get the project done faster. In essence, using a framework may cause your final products to look like the framework. Sometimes, this may not be such a terrible notion, that is, having a toolset at your disposal that helps you develop faster and better websites. There are many frameworks available; some are bare-bones, and require that you invest more time in design and development but you have more control over the final product; conversely, some provide more features, but the framework guides your design and it will be difficult to change without a full redesign.

So, which framework is right for you? The answer is of course; it depends on what is best for the project requirements. I suggest trying out the recipes in this chapter and having a number of tools at your disposal and ready to build with.

Using the Fluid 960 grid layout

The **960 Grid System** has been around for a while and has already proven useful in deploying new projects quickly. It is fairly simple to learn, and after a quick learning curve you can jump right into using it.

The only snag in this is that it is not responsive. In fact, it behaves much like a table using column, spanned over fixed-width table headers. It lays out nicely in a 960px-wide window, and that's it, you are stuck with a good view in only one browser window size. So why even discuss the 960 grid at all in a book about responsive design? The answer is that some people liked it so much that they decided to fix the problem.

Getting ready

There are good solutions for this, and hopefully you can find them in this chapter. Bear with me and I'll show you one of the simpler versions of it in this recipe. The simple responsive version of 960 Grid System could actually be more accurately described as a **fluid grid**. It replaces much of the fixed-width grid elements with percentage width, left-floating element. This works pretty well but when the columns get narrow, it can become difficult to read. We can fix this rather easily with some additional CSS.

What we eventually want for our page is to respond to the screen changes by exerting more granular change over how the grid is laid out in different screen sizes.

First, go get the Fluid 960 Grid System at `http://www.designinfluences.com/fluid960gs/`. Then, download and expand the archived files. Copy the `grid.css` file from the archived `CSS` folder into your project's `CSS` folder. Next, create a new CSS file in your `CSS` directory called `responsive.css`. We'll come back to that later.

How to do it...

Create a new HTML file in your IDE. Add links to the file `grid.css`, and to your new CSS file, `responsive.css`:

```
<link rel="stylesheet" href="css/grid.css" media="screen" />
<link rel="stylesheet" href="css/responsive.css" media="screen" />
```

Next, create some content within your HTML body. Then, to make the Fluid 960 Grid work, you first add a wrapping `div` element with a class to define the number of columns inside it. For this recipe use the class `containter_16`, for a total of 16 usable columns. You also have the option of having 12 columns by assigning to the `div` element the `container_12` class.

Inside the `container_16` element, first create a container for a header. Create a new `div` element with a class `grid_16`. You probably have already guessed that the `grid_16` class takes the whole width of the `container_16` div. That was a pretty good guess; you are 98 percent correct; it actually takes 98 percent of the width, or all 16 columns with 2 percent outer padding. If you had instead used the `grid_11` class it would have taken up 11 columns, or 66.75 percent with 2 percent padding on the outside.

To create a new line, we add the another `div` element, this time with the class `clear`. This works in a similar way to the _Enter_ key on your keyboard, or a newline (\n) in some programming languages. This `clear` element is necessary between rows because their position is set by a `left:float` property, which does not have a vertical space.

```
<div class="clear"></div>
```

The same could be accomplished by using an uncomplicated break, as follows:

```
<br class="clear">
```

You will need to add the `clear` div or break between every row.

Now, we will focus onto the content! Following your `clear` element, add six new `div` elements. Give the first element a `grid_3` class, the second element the `grid_5` class, and the rest of the elements the `grid_2` class. The order does not matter, as long as the number following the `grid_*` adds up to 16. Insert a few lines of Ipsum filler text (`http://lipsum.com`) inside the `div` elements. Your code will look something like this:

```
<div class="container_16">
<div class="grid_16">
<h2>Fluid Grid</h2>
</div>
<div class="clear"></div>
<div class="grid_3">Loremipsum dolor sit amet...</div>
<div class="grid_5">Curabitursapien ante, pretium...</div>
<div class="grid_2">tiam quam tortor, necsagittis ...</div>
<div class="grid_2">Donecmollisconsequatarcuvel...</div>
<div class="grid_2">Nullam sit amet magna dui. In dictum...</div>
<div class="grid_2">Etiamsuscipitvariuspharetra...</div>
</div>
```

In the following screenshot, you can see how the fluid grid breaks down on smaller viewports:

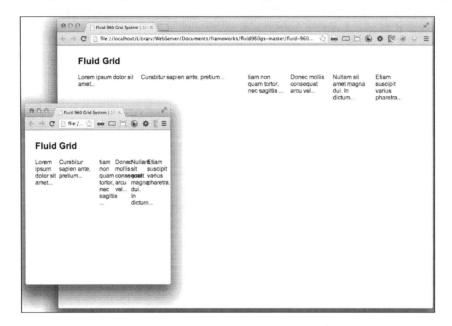

The next step is to update your CSS to add some responsiveness to the fluid layout. Now, open your `responsive.css` file in your IDE to edit it. Add media queries to cover the smaller screen breakpoints: `1024px`, `600px`, and `420px`, as shown in the following code snippet:

```
@media screen and (max-width:420px){...}
@media screen and (max-width:600px) and (min-width:421px){...}
@media screen and (max-width:1024px) and (min-width:601px){...}
```

Our intent is to make some new CSS that will override the fluid grid and make new sticking breakpoints for content elements. At narrower widths we want an element to have a greater percentage width, or a fixed width. To make the override, we will add a new class to the media queries: `.break-column`.

Next add to the `max-width:420px` media query a `min-width` value of `360px` for the `.break-column` element class. Then, add to the new media queries, `max-width:600px` and `min-width:421px`, add the `.grid_2.break-column`, `.grid_3.break-column`, and `.grid_5.break-column` element classes and their `width:48%` property. In the largest of the three media queries, add the class with a property of `width:30%` followed by the `!important` override (be sure it is inserted before the semicolon), as shown in the following code snippet:

```
@media screen and (max-width:420px){
    .break-column{min-width:360px;}
}
```

```
@media screen and (min-width:421px) and (max-width:600px){
    .grid_2.break-column, .grid_3.break-column, .grid_5.break-
column{width:48%;}
}
@media screen and (max-width:1024px) and (min-width:601px){
    .break-column{width:30% !important;}
}
```

One last step to a responsive fluid grid! Open your HTML file again and add to each of the six div elements a class of break-column. And the recipe is complete. Refresh your browser, or open the HTML to view it. As you scale down your browser window or open the file in a mobile device, you will see the layout responds with a more optimized layout for the smaller views. The fluid grid is illustrated in the following screenshot:

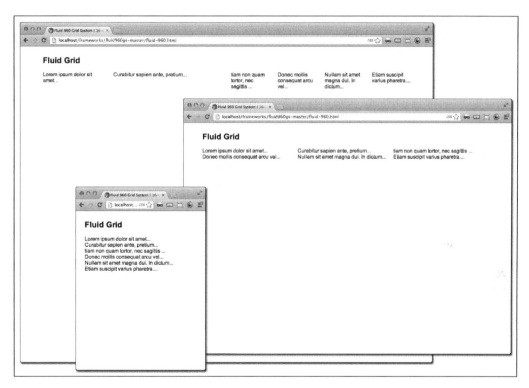

How it works...

When you open the un-updated (fluid and non-responsive) HTML file in your browser, you will see your six columns, and they will fluidly retain their same proportional width as the browser window or the device gets smaller. When viewed in a small window or mobile device, it will display six unreadable narrow columns.

Adding the media queries works by overriding the style properties of the `div` elements. I demonstrated overrides with three different methods: first, the `min-width` method overrides the percent width; next, as the `responsive.css` file follows the `grid.css` file and the CSS is explicitly name-spaced (`.grid_2.break-column`, `.grid_3.break-column`, and `.grid_5.break-column`), it overrides the fluid width declared in the `grid.css` file, and in the last case, the `!important` declaration trumps all in the override cascade.

Using the Blueprint grid layout

The **Blueprint CSS** framework is another popular static CSS grid system. There may be a case where you come across a need to make the static Blueprint CSS grid framework into your very own responsive Blueprint framework. This one is pretty easy to break apart into a responsive layout. There are only a few simple CSS breaks to insert and you have a responsive framework.

Getting ready

First go and get a hold of the Blueprint CSS framework. You can download it at `http://www.blueprintcss.org/`. This framework works similarly to other static CSS grid frameworks.

How to do it....

Once you have downloaded the Blueprint framework, extract the files and copy the `blueprint` folder into your `CSS` directory. Next we'll start building the HTML file to work with the Blueprint CSS framework. Create a new HTML file in your IDE. Inside the body, add a title, and then an `hr` element.

"Huh? A what?", you may ask. It's a horizontal rule—a thematic break. Let me explain.

In previous versions of HTML, `hr` was a horizontal rule. Meaning it acted like a break, but places a horizontal line across the page. It got an upgrade in HTML5, and is now a thematic break. So what's the difference? It still, by itself, does the same thing putting a horizontal line across the page. However, in the past it was used to define the layout, but now it emphasizes a change in theme or content.

However, in Blueprint CSS, the `hr` element is used specifically to capture a row. Okay? Let us get back to our task at hand.

After your `hr` element, you can start a row of content. First create a three-column layout for the first row. Then, insert some Ipsum (`http://Ipsum.com`) text into the three `div` elements. This, like the 960 Grid, works like a table `colspan`, you assign a class to the `div` element corresponding to the number of columns you want the element to span across. The total number of columns is 22. The first three classes will be: `span-7`, `span-8`, and `span-7`. Follow the same steps with another thematic break:

```
<h1>Blueprint CSS Framework Responsive<h2>
<hr>
  <div class="span-7">Loremipsum dolor sit amet,
   consecteturadipiscingelit...</div>
  <div class="span-8">Etiamegettortorlectus, et
   variusnibh...</div>
  <div class="span-7">Duis sit
   ametfelislobortisfeliscommodolacinia...</div>
<hr>
```

In your next row, add two large columns. Add two divs with the classes `span-15` and `span-7` in them. In the left-hand side `div` element, add a paragraph of Ipsum text and an image. In the right-hand side column, add an unordered list of Ipsum text sentences. Then close the row with a horizontal rule:

```
<hr />
<div class="span-15">
    <img src="test.jpg" class="top pull-1 left" alt="test">
    <p>Loremipsum dolor sit amet, consectetueradipiscingelit...</p>
</div>
<div class="span-7">
<ul>
<li>Loremipsum dolor sit amet, consectetueradipiscingelit...</li>
<li>Loremipsum dolor sit amet, consectetueradipiscingelit...</li>
<li>Loremipsum dolor sit amet, consectetueradipiscingelit...</li>
</ul>
</div>
<hr />
```

This is most of the HTML we want to build for this recipe. If you want more, you can see the `sample.html` file in the `tests` folder of the archive you downloaded.

In your HTML header, add links to the Blueprint CSS framework stylesheets in the `css/Blueprint/` directory.

Next, let's add our own stylesheet to make the framework a responsive one. Add a new link to the new stylesheet, `responsive.css`, in your header. If you have not already added the CSS file, then add the new `responsive.css` stylesheet:

```
<link rel="stylesheet" href="css/responsive.css"  >
```

Open the `responsive.css` stylesheet. Create a media query for the smallest breakpoint, and for the next breakpoint. Make the media query breakpoints at `600px` and `1024px`, as follows:

```
@media screen and (max-width:600px) {...}
@media screen and (min-width:601px) and (max-width:1024px) {...}
```

Inside it we're going to use a CSS trick called an **attribute selector**. This is like using a wildcard `*`. To make a property apply to all of the column span classes in the Blueprint CSS grid, such as span-1, span-2, span-3, and more, you write it like this: `div[class*='span']{...}`. This is a wonderful trick for making responsive overrides in a CSS grid.

At the `600px` media query, add CSS with the attribute selector, and add a width of `90%`. This will make all the spans expand to 100 percent when the browser window is less than `600px` wide. Do the same in the `1024px` media query with a width of `42%`. If you were expecting nice round numbers such as 100 percent and 50 percent, you may be surprised; but keep in mind that Blueprint CSS adds padding already.

```
@media screen and (max-width:600px) {
    div[class*='span-']{width:90%;}
}
@media screen and (min-width:601px) and (max-width:1024px) {
    div[class*='span-']{width:42%;}
}
```

Open the HTML in your browser or refresh your screen and you'll see that when you change the browser width, the spans adjust automatically to the new width.

You may notice that the second row leaves too much white space when you hit that `1024px` breakpoint. Let's fix that. Copy your attribute selector CSS line in the `1024px` media query and paste it beneath. Append a `.wide` class to the attribute selector. Give it a width of `90%`.

In your HTML file add a `wide` class to the first span after the second thematic break (`hr`), the one with the image inside it.

This works great on the most recent browsers, but not yet in old browsers. We'll need to add just a few lines of CSS to make this work in more browsers. In your `responsive.css` file, add on the first line the class `.container`, and give the attribute a width of `960px`. Then inside each media query add the same class, but change the width to `100%`.

```
.container{width:960px}
@media screen and (max-width:600px) {
        div[class*='span-']{width:90%;}
        .container{width:100%}
}
```

```
@media screen and (min-width:601px) and (max-width:1024px){
     div[class*='span-']{width:42%;}
     div[class*='span-'].wide{width:90%;}
     .container{width:100%}
}
```

That will help it from breaking in older browsers that don't support media queries.

For some extra fun, add some CSS3 transition to the spans. This will make a smooth animated transition to the width of the affected spans. Do this outside of any media queries.

```
div[class*='span-']{

-moz-transition: width 0.1s; /* Firefox 4 */
-webkit-transition: width 0.1s; /* Safari and Chrome */
-o-transition: width 0.1s; /* Opera */
transition: width 0.1s;

}
```

With this extra tidbit you can do some fancier responsive design in each media query. The new responsive Blueprint is illustrated in the following screenshot:

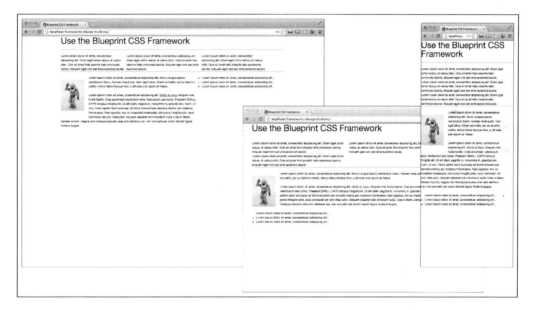

How it works...

To make the Blueprint CSS framework responsive, we first changed its container width from a static width to a fluid maximum width, and added media queries at breakpoints. The key ingredient in this recipe was the attribute selector that allowed us to throw a wildcard at the CSS and avoid having to recode each span's property.

Fluid layout using the rule of thirds

The **rule of thirds** is a design methodology that states that a layout or an image can be made more interesting if it is divided into three parts horizontally or vertically. And like everything else related to the Internet, there is endless discussion and debate on it. For the purpose of this book, all we care about is how to make it useful.

There is no indexed in search results, at least that I've seen, responsive and fluid layout based on the rule of thirds. However, there is a good static framework based on the Rule of Thirds. It's called the **Golden Grid**.

Getting ready

Search for `Golden Grid`, and `http://code.google.com/p/the-golden-grid/` should be the first result. From the top navigation, go to the **Downloads** page and get the latest version.

How to do it...

Look inside the extracted files for a `CSS/golden-base` directory. Inside it, copy the `golden.css` file into your development directory. You will use this CSS file as your base framework for layout.

In a new HTML file add a link to the `golden.css` stylesheet.

```
<link rel="stylesheet" href="CSS/golden.css" media="screen,
projection">
```

Open this CSS file and edit the property of the `.main` class. Change `width:970px` to `max-width:970px`. This will break the static page template and allow the outer wrap to adjust as the browser's window shrinks.

While you have the `golden.css` stylesheet open, take a look at how this works. It's very simple; three vertical lines, and then for each division divide the page layout by half, and then in half again. The class spans start at `70px` width with the `80px` increments until they fill up their `width:950px;` attribute. To assign the `width` property to your element, assign it a class starting with the letter `g` plus the width and `10px` for a margin. These also have the `float:left;` and `display:inline;` styles. Because they are left-floating inline elements, when they run out of horizontal room, they will take a new line. Since they are left floated, they are aligned left, to move them to the right, you can either put empty elements in front of it, or use the framework's `.margin` class to put a left margin in front of it.

The margins work much like the grid span's widths, they increment by `80px`, the only difference is that they start at `90px` instead of `70px`. The difference is accounted for in the element's `margin-left:10px` property.

The elements line up in rows, and like the other frameworks we have worked with them in this chapter, it uses an element to clear the end of the row, before starting a new one. In this case, the framework uses a div with a `clear:both` property.

Let's now get back to editing the HTML file and create a responsive layout using the Rule of Thirds. We will start by creating a static layout. Create a header (`H1`) with a style of `width:100%`, and then add three divs to clear new rows.

```
<body>
<div class="g960"><h1>Golden Grid CSS Layout</h1></div>
    <div class="clear"></div>
    <div class="clear"></div>
    <div class="clear"></div>
</body>
```

After the first clearing `div` element, add a `div` element with the class `.g960`, and we will insert a large image in which we will create responsiveness characteristics. You can refer to the *Resizing an image using percent width* recipe in *Chapter 1, Responsive Elements and Media*, for a refresher on to making images responsive:

```
<div class="clear"></div>
<div class="g960">
<img src="robot-large.png" class="resp" alt="robot picture"/>
</div>
<div class="clear"></div>
```

After the next break, insert six `div` elements, each with the class `g160`. Inside each, insert a paragraph of Ipsum text. For a more informative example, replace one of the `.g160` elements with an 80px-wide class. Be sure to also include the class for the margin, `ml80`, as follows:

```
<div class="clear"></div>
<div class="g160"><p>Loremipsum dolor sit amet...</p></div>
<div class="g160"><p>Loremipsum dolor sit amet...</p></div>
<div class="g160"><p>Loremipsum dolor sit amet...</p></div>
<div class="g160"><p>Loremipsum dolor sit amet...</p></div>
<div class="g80 ml80"><p>Loremipsum dolor sit amet...</p></div>
<div class="g160"><p>Loremipsum dolor sit amet...</p></div>
<div class="clear"></div>
```

That's likely enough for the HTML to get a clear demonstration of how to make this work. Let us now move on to adding our CSS to make this a responsive design.

Add a new CSS file to your CSS directory, `responsive.css`, and link to it in your HTML head.

```
<link rel="stylesheet" href="CSS/responsive.css" media="screen,
projection">
```

Here, we'll add some CSS properties to make the CSS framework responsive. First, let's take care of that large image. We'd rather not let it stay large when the browser gets smaller.

```
.resp{
    width:100%;
    height:auto;
}
```

Next, add media queries at two breakpoints, `600px` for mobile and `1024px` for tablets. You can add more as you like for larger screens, but for this recipe we're just covering the basics.

```
@media screen and (max-width:600px){...}
@media screen and (min-width:601px) and (max-width:1024px){...}
```

For all screens smaller than `600px`, we want all the `div` elements to default to the full width of the screen. Do not forget that we have classes with left-margin properties; we'll want to shrink those to zero. To keep the new CSS minimal, let's use the CSS attribute selectors to wildcard select all the grid classes. Add `div[class*='g']{...}` and assign a width of `90%`, and `div[class*='ml']  {...}` to assign a left margin of `0`.

```
@media screen and (max-width:600px){
    div[class*='g']{width:96%;}
    div[class*='ml']{margin-left:0;}
}
```

For screens ranging from 600px to 1024px, add the same but change the grid class' width to 48%. For this @media query, we don't want every element to drop to half of the screen. That would kill all of the joy of this responsive framework. After your attribute selector, add .wide to make a distinct CSS property for this distinct class. Then, give it a width of 96%. In your HTML, add the wide class to the title and the image parent div elements (they are the elements with the g960 class).

```
div[class*='g'].wide{width:96%;}
```

The following screenshot illustrates the Golden Grid behavior:

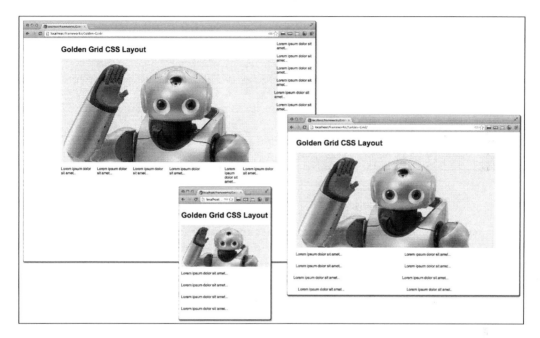

How it works...

The attribute selectors give us a tidy trick to break apart a rigid framework across limited column spans into a full width across the screen. Combine this with your custom media queries to only change the HTML on smaller screens, and you have an easy recipe for a responsive, and potentially visually, compelling layout for all sizes. This same technique can be used for a number of different frameworks.

There's more...

Let's have some fun and take this a little further. We've so far in this chapter dealt mostly with making static frameworks that run on a mobile device. Let's do an experiment together to make the Golden Grid do something cool when displayed on a large screen. Add a new media query for the `1280px` breakpoint.

```
@media screen and (min-width:1280px){...}
```

This extra section of the recipe goes a little deeper into attribute selectors. It may be a bit disturbing at first to see basic logic in your CSS, but bear with me and you'll find some new tools for your toolbox, which you will find very useful. But, first let's add some more content and an HTML structure.

Copy the last row of your HTML and append it to the HTML page right after where you have copied it. Give it a parent `div` element with a class of `g960`. To the preceding `div` element, add the class `last clear`.

```
<div class="last clear"></div>
<div class="g960">
    <div class="g160"><p>Loremipsum dolor sit amet...</p></div>
    <div class="g160"><p>Loremipsum dolor sit amet...</p></div>
    <div class="g160"><p>Loremipsum dolor sit amet...</p></div>
    <div class="g160"><p>Loremipsum dolor sit amet...</p></div>
    <div class="g80 ml80"><p>Loremipsum dolor sit amet...</p></div>
    <div class="g160"><p>Loremipsum dolor sit amet...</p></div>
</div>
```

Back to your CSS. The attribute selectors now allow more conditions, such as parents, children, and precedence. Let's use this to apply CSS properties to the grid element preceded by the `.last` div. To do this we use a ~ symbol; the syntax is as follows:

```
DIV.preceding~DIV.following
```

We want this element to change into a column on the right-hand side when the screen is bigger than 1280px to maximize our viewing area.

```
div.last~div[class*='g']{position:absolute;right:0;top:0;width:14%;max-width:226px;}
```

Next, we want all its children to line up nicely and take up the available space, as well as remove any margins from the `ml` classes. This syntax is much like the preceding one, but uses a > symbol; and is written like this `DIV.parent>DIV.child`.

```
div.last~div[class*='g']>div[class*='g']{display:block;float:none;width:100%;}
div.last~div[class*='g']>div[class*='ml']{margin-left:0;}
```

We also need to prevent the wrapping `g960` grid element from being affected by the wildcard in the `max-width:1024px` media query. Add the same attribute selector to the grid div element preceded by the `.last` div element and give it a width of `100%`, this is shown in the following code line:

```
div.last~div[class*='g']{width:100%}
```

Now refresh your browser's window and expand it past the `1280px` breakpoint. You'll see that the last row move into a sidebar position. Who says frameworks are too rigid to be responsive?

Now, you already know that media queries are not supported in old browsers, so since we care for all of our audience we want to give some love to the steadfast users of old browsers. Copy the CSS from the `1280px` media query breakpoint, and add it to a pre IE9-only stylesheet. Then make a conditional link to the stylesheet in your header:

```
<!--[if lt IE 9]>
  <link rel="stylesheet" type="text/css" href="IE8.css" />
<![endif]-->
```

This will take care of the old-browser-support issues and your site will still look good in the older browsers.

Trying Gumby, a responsive 960 grid

The Gumby framework is a continued effort on the good old reliable static 960 Grid framework. It was brought to you by the nice folks at Digital Surgeons. The framework itself has been updated, and a good number of bells and whistles have been added. There are, of course more features than we have time to go through in this recipe, so we're going to stick solely to the improved layout structure of the framework.

Getting ready

Let's take a look at the Gumby 960 Responsive framework's website `gumbyframework. com/`. As you go through it, you can see the modernized framework features in action. The layout snaps nicely to a mobile version at 767px, and in addition transforms the menu into a usable mobile navigation. There are several useful UI elements included that you will want to spend some time to getting familiar with.

Click on the highly prominent **Download Gumby 2** button on the navigation to acquire the Gumby's master version archive. Included inside the package are Photoshop files to help you design your layout, the actual framework CSS, JavaScript, image files, and sample HTML files. The `demo.html` file could be a good place to examine the source and make some discoveries about how the framework is used.

But save the poking around for later, let's jump right into building a page.

How to do it...

Start by creating a new page in your HTML editor. This framework has a lean method of importing in your CSS scripts inside a singular link to `css/imports.css`. Inside that file, the different stylesheets are imported. This is a helpful concept in case you need to change or add stylesheets in the future, you can control it in this CSS file.

```
<link rel="stylesheet" href="css/imports.css">
```

This is what the CSS looks like:

```
@import url('gumby.hybrid.css');
@import url('ui.css');
@import url('style.css');
@import url('text.css');
```

Just so you don't forget, add your links to a jQuery library and the included JavaScript files: `gumby.min.js`, `plugins.js`, and `main.js`, at the end of the page directly before the closing body tag. You will need these later.

```
<script src="http://ajax.googleapis.com/ajax/libs/jquery/1.7.2/jquery.
min.js"></script>
<script src="js/libs/gumby.min.js"></script>
<script src="js/plugins.js"></script>
<script src="js/main.js"></script>
</body>
```

Now that the basics are taken care of, let's move on to some development. The Gumby Responsive Grid framework can use either 12 or 16 columns. Start with building a 12-column layout and later we will make the page a hybrid one by adding a 16-layer section.

Inside your HTML body, add a `div` element with the class `container`. The default layout inside the `container` class element is 12 columns. Next, inside the `container` class element, add a new `div` element with a `row` class assigned. The `row` class element encapsulates each entire range of the 12 column spans. Inside each row, you have 12 column spans to work with, to build your content divs with.

Insert inside the `row` class element three new div elements with classes, `four columns`, `three columns`, and `five columns`. The column classes can be of whatever number your design requires, as long as they together are equal to 12. The number label of the class determines the number of column spans the element occupies. Inside each of these elements add a paragraph of Ipsum filler text (`http://ipsum.com`), to help give a more illustrative demonstration of the layout.

```
<div class="container">
        <div class="row">
```

```
<div class="four columns"><p>Loremipsum dolor sit amet,
consecteturadipiscingelit. ...</p></div>
<div class="three columns"><p>Loremipsum dolor sit amet,
consecteturadipiscingelit. ...</p></div>
<div class="five columns"><p>Loremipsum dolor sit amet,
consecteturadipiscingelit. ...</p></div>
        </div>
</div>
```

Feel free to launch this page in your browser now and see how it looks. Test its responsiveness to see how it behaves on the smaller screens. The CSS for the class, columns, looks as follows:

```
.column, .columns {
margin-left: 2.127663%;
float: left;
min-height: 1px;
position: relative;
-webkit-box-sizing: border-box;
-moz-box-sizing: border-box;
box-sizing: border-box;
}
```

The CSS for the number classes look as follows:

```
.row .two.columns {
width: 14.893641%;
}
.row .three.columns {
width: 23.404293%;
}
.row .four.columns {
width: 31.914945%;
}
.row .five.columns {
width: 40.425597%;
}
....
And so on.
```

As you can see, the columns class gives a relative position and floats the element to the left, with padding and some other style.

Next add another `div` element with the `row` class. And inside the `row` div, add a row of the six smaller `div` elements. Each of the new `div` elements will have the classes, `two` and `columns`. These together will take up a span of 12 columns. Include a short paragraph of text inside each element.

```
<div class="row">
<div class="two columns"><p>Loremipsum dolor sit amet...</p></div>
<div class="two columns"><p>Cum sociisnatoquepenatibus et...</p></div>
<div class="two columns"><p>eufacilisis sem. Phasellus...</p></div>
<div class="two columns"><p>Loremipsum dolor sit amet...</p></div>
<div class="two columns"><p>Cum sociisnatoquepenatibus et...</p></div>
<div class="two columns"><p>eufacilisis sem. Phasellus...</p></div>
</div>
```

In your browser, you can see that these align nicely into six columns of content. When you go to a small browser window, you will see that they jump to 100 percent width.

So far, the grids work in an orderly fashion if you have designed all your element to float against the left-hand side of the screen. However, that is not always the case; there will always be uses for content to be right, center, or some other arbitrary alignment. Don't worry, the Gumby 960 Responsive framework has thought of that. Let's add some more rows that demonstrate how to do that.

In the first row, we'll make two `div` elements, one on the left-hand side, and one on the right-hand side. Add a new `row` div element, and inside it, add two more `div` elements. Give the first one, which will lie on the left-hand side of the screen, the classes `two` and `columns`. With these two classes, the first `div` element floats left and spans across two columns. We want the next `div` element to only take up six columns, give it the classes, `six` and `columns`. We do not want this next column to float towards the left; instead, it should have some space between the previous `div` element and itself. To make this, there is a series of classes that have only a set percentage left-margin. In this case, we need to push the element four column spans to the right. To do so add the class, `push_four`.

```
<div class="row">
<div class="two columns"><p>Loremipsum dolor sit amet...</p></div>
<div class="six columns push_four"><p>Consecteturadipiscingeli...</p>/
div>
</div>
```

The following is the CSS for the `push_four` class:

```
.row .push_four {
margin-left: 36.170271%;
}
```

To make a column span of content *centered*, there is a special class for that. I put center in quotes, because it's not really centered, it's pseudo-centered. Instead of using a `text-align:center` or `float:center` property, the Gumby Grid uses a smart left-margin system. The CSS for the centered `six column` div element looks as follows:

```
.row .six.centered {
margin-left: 25.531956%;
}
```

It follows the same pattern as the number classes, a centered `five column` row has a greater left margin: `margin-left: 29.787282%`.

Finally, before we end this recipe, let's make use the framework to build a responsive menu. This is worth the little extra time to show at least one of the responsive UI elements included in the framework.

Since the CSS is already built we'll just go through the HTML to build this menu. Back at the top of the `container` div element, add a `row` div element. In the `row` div element add a `nav` element with the `id` value of "prettynav" and the `pretty navbarclearfix` class. Next, inside the `nav` element, add an `a href` tag with a `link` value equal to #, a `toggle` class, and a `data-for` value as #prettynav>ul element tag. Instead of text inside the `a href` element, add the image inside that is included in the `img` directory, `img/icon_nav_toggle.gif`.

```
<div class="row">
<nav class="pretty navbarclearfix" id="prettynav">
<a href="#" class="toggle" data-for="#prettynav&gt; ul"><img src="img/
icon_nav_toggle.gif"></a>
</nav>
</div>
```

The `a href` element works as a button to display the navigation menu, when it is hidden in the mobile version of the menu.

Following the `a href` element, add an unordered list (`ul`) with list items (`li`) that contain the links of your navigation:

```
<ul>
  <li><a href="#">First Item</a></li>
  <li><a href="#">Second Item</a></li>
  <li><a href="#">Third Item</a></li>
  <li><a href="#">Fourth Item</a></li>
</ul>
```

This alone creates a nice responsive menu system and that would be exciting enough, but there's still more. You can add a submenu to each one of those menu list items. To add one submenu, add a `div` element with a class `dropdown`. Inside that `div` element, add a submenu `ul` with list items similar to the parent. They automatically are converted to a hidden submenu!

```
<li>
<a href="#">Second Item</a>
<div class="dropdown">
<ul>
<li><a href="#">Dropdown item</a></li>
<li><a href="#">Dropdown item</a></li>
</ul>
</div>
</li>
```

The following screenshot illustrates the Gumby framework:

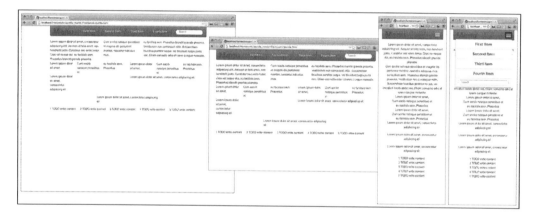

How it works...

The Gumby 960 Grid framework was designed and built to be an elegant and easy layout and element framework. There is not much needed to know how to make it work. First, learn how to class your `div` elements to make them work within the framework. Secondly, build it. Understanding how to use the UI elements included in the framework will require some more involvement, but it will be well worth your time.

The Bootstrap framework makes responsive layouts easy

The Bootstrap framework (formerly known as the **Twitter Bootstrap** framework) stands out from most other frameworks, as it is completely responsive out of the box. You can either use it as a static framework, or use their additional files to quickly deploy a fully responsive site. This is a great tool to use when you need to produce fast and good sites, and you are willing to make minimal design adjustments to an external standard.

Acquiring the framework is as easy as searching for `Bootstrap Framework` and going to the first link, `http://twitter.github.com/bootstrap/`, and clicking on the big **Download Bootstrap** button. The package includes CSS files, images, and JavaScript, but no documentation. There is, however, plenty of good documentation online at their site, and the source of their examples is highly coherent. This recipe will get you started along the path of using the Bootstrap framework.

Getting ready

Building with the Bootstrap framework is remarkably easy; you can get a template spun up in a matter of minutes. That being said, let's push through it. Spin up a new HTML file and get started. First, add a link in your header to the Bootstrap CSS files so we can on occasion see our work in action:

```
<link href="css/bootstrap.css" rel="stylesheet" media="screen">
<link href="css/bootstrap-responsive.css" rel="stylesheet"
media="screen">
```

Let us start with a simple page with a top navigation and content. The navigation will respond to the screen's width and optimize for each display. The navigation `div` element uses several classes to achieve the desired results; they are `navbarnavbar-inverse navbar-fixed-top`. Inside it, add a `div` element with the class `container`. Inside the `container` div element, there is a button graphic that is displayed in the mobile version. When clicked, it displays the mobile version of the menu. The menu is displayed in an optimized manner for both mobile and desktop versions. Pretty cool, eh!

Following is a sample menu to show how it is put together:

```
<div class="navbarnavbar-inverse navbar-fixed-top">
    <div class="navbar-inner">
      <div class="container">
```

```
          <a class="btnbtn-navbar" data-toggle="collapse" data-
target=".nav-collapse">
            <span class="icon-bar"></span>
            <span class="icon-bar"></span>
            <span class="icon-bar"></span>
          </a>
          <a class="brand" href="#">Project name</a>
          <div class="nav-collapse collapse">
            <ul class="nav">
              <li class="active"><a href="#">Home</a></li>
              <li><a href="#about">About</a></li>
              <li><a href="#contact">Contact</a></li>
            </ul>
          </div><!--/.nav-collapse -->
        </div>
      </div>
    </div>
```

Then, insert into your header, a link to the jQuery library.

```
<script src="http://code.jquery.com/jquery-latest.min.js" ></script>
```

Then, at the bottom of your HTML, right before the closing `body` tag, add a link to the `js/bootstrap.js` file.

```
<script src="js/bootstrap.js"></script>
```

Finally, if you haven't already copied the JS directly into your `webroot`, do so.

Now, check your slick responsive navigation.

That was great, wasn't it? Now that we're both excited about the Bootstrap framework, let's get to work on some responsive content layout. Next, let's go through and build what Bootstrap calls a basic marketing site.

First thing to do is add a `div` element with the `container` class. If you look back at our menu, you'll find that this class is a clever re-usable layout element used throughout, to control the responsive width of the containing elements. Inside the `container` element, add a new `div` element and give it a class, `hero-unit`. Inside the `hero-unit` class, add some content that you want to display in a large billboard style on the screen:

```
<div class="container">
<div class="hero-unit">
<h1>Hello World</h1>
<p>Loremipsum dolor sit amet...</p>
</div>
</div>
```

Refresh your browser and try that on for size. Everything looks great without much effort. Beneath that we want to add some columns of the teaser text. This is starting to look like a good landing page. Aren't you glad you are doing this?

The Bootstrap framework uses a `div` element with a `row` class to outline its column spans. So to create a new *row* of content, add a new `div` element with the `row` class. Inside the row you have 12 spans available to work your content into. For this recipe, let's stick with simple, so insert three new `div` elements, each with a `span4` class, inside the `row` div element. Inside each `span4` element, add a secondary header and a paragraph of Ipsum (`http://lipsum.com`) filler text.

```
<div class="row">
<div class="span4">
<h2>Header</h2>
<p>Loremipsum dolor sit amet, consecteturadipiscingelit...</p>
</div>
<div class="span4">
<h2>Header</h2>
<p>Loremipsum dolor sit amet, consecteturadipiscingelit...</p>
</div>
<div class="span4">
<h2>Header</h2>
<p>Loremipsum dolor sit amet, consecteturadipiscingelit......</p>
</div>
```

Open up your browser window or refresh it and see this nice layout in action. The newest row takes up three columns and collapses nicely into a single column, when you go to a mobile browser or windows with a smaller widths.

You could copy the entire `row` class element and inner HTML, and paste it to add a whole new row of content, and it will behave nicely.

Now that we have made a good looking page and it did not take any earth-shattering exertion, let us add another level to the page. This part is an excellent demonstration of the flexibility of the Bootstrap framework. Next, you are going to add a side navigation to the page.

In the second `container` class element, wrap the `hero-unit` and `row` elements in a new `div` element and assign that element a `span9` class. Next, insert before your new element another `div` element with the class `span3`. That should take care of the change in layout of the page; next we are going to rapidly build a menu inside it.

Add a new `div` element inside your `span3` div class, and give it the classes: `well` and `sidebar-nav`. These give the sidebar navigation a good-looking style. Now, onto the menu list, add an unordered list (`ul`) with the classes, `nav` and `nav-list`. You can add list section headers by assigning a class `nav-header` to a list item. Add in each of the list items, a `href` link for the navigation items:

```
<div class="well sidebar-nav">
    <ul class="navnav-list">
        <li class="nav-header">Navigation 1</li>
        <li><a href="#">Nav Link</a></li>
        <li><a href="#">Nav Link</a></li>
        <li><a href="#">Nav Link</a></li>
        <li class="nav-header">Navigation 2</li>
        <li><a href="#">Nav Link</a></li>
        <li><a href="#">Nav Link</a></li>
        <li><a href="#">Nav Link</a></li>
    </ul>
</div>
```

You're almost done; there are only a couple of more steps in this recipe. Wrap your two new `span*` elements in another `div` element with a `row` or `row-fluid` class. Finally, change the `row` div element class name that contains the teaser content's elements to `row-fluid`.

```
<div class="container">
        <div class="row">
          <div class="span3">
          <div class="well sidebar-nav">
            <ul class="navnav-list">
              <li class="nav-header">Navigation 1</li>
              <li><a href="#">Nav Link</a></li>
              <li><a href="#">Nav Link</a></li>
              <li><a href="#">Nav Link</a></li>
              <li class="nav-header">Navigation 2</li>
              <li><a href="#">Nav Link</a></li>
                  <li><a href="#">Nav Link</a></li>
                  <li><a href="#">Nav Link</a></li>
              </ul>
          </div>

        </div>
        <div class="span9">
        <div class="hero-unit">
  <h1>Hello World</h1>
      <p>Loremipsum dolor sit amet, consecteturadipiscingelit...</p>
        </div>
          <div class="row-fluid">
          <div class="span4">
            <h2>Header</h2>
            <p>Loremipsum dolor sit amet, consectetur adipiscing
  elit...</p>
```

```
        </div>
        <div class="span4">
          <h2>Header</h2>
          <p>Loremipsum dolor sit amet,
consecteturadipiscingelit...</p>
        </div>
      </div>
    </div>
  </div>

</div>
```

Congratulations, you are done! You now have a firm base to a professional-looking responsive layout and design. You could only make a few modifications to this and have a finished product. The following screenshot shows the base Bootstrap framework:

Like magic! No really, the Bootstrap framework has to be one of the easiest and well thought-out frameworks I've worked with yet. Once you go through the recipe and their documentation to get familiar with the classes and layout, it's very easy to rapidly develop your projects.

There are some specific items I want to discuss. First the responsive menu; the top `div` element inside the `container` class is `button`, which is displayed only in the mobile version, and its purpose is, when clicked, to reveal the hidden menu `div` element, `nav-collapse`, in a mobile style.

This, by itself, gives you a great starter for a usable and very elegant responsive menu. However, you will find that the button does not work by itself, that's because we need to add some JavaScript to make this battle-station fully operational.

The responsive layout does heavy lifting behind the scenes for you also. Each row of the columns you create takes up the specified columns, but collapses nicely into a single column when you go to a mobile browser, or a window with small width.

There's more...

There is so much more you can do with this framework. There are rich elements, menus, UI functions, and animations galore included in the Bootstrap framework. Take some time and get a more in-depth understanding of the framework and you will be happy you did. After learning this I found that I could deploy new work much more quickly and with a much less frustrating process.

104

5
Making Mobile-first Web Applications

In this chapter, you will learn about:

- ▶ Using the Safari Developer Tools' User Agent switcher
- ▶ Masking your user agent in Chrome with a plugin
- ▶ Using browser resizing plugins
- ▶ Learning the viewport and its options
- ▶ Adding tags for jQuery Mobile
- ▶ Adding a second page in jQuery Mobile
- ▶ Making a list element in jQuery Mobile
- ▶ Adding a mobile native-looking button with jQuery Mobile
- ▶ Adding a mobile stylesheet for mobile browsers only using the media query
- ▶ Adding JavaScript for mobile browsers only

Introduction

In this chapter, we will focus our efforts on mobile-first Responsive Design. By this, we mean first designing your site for the mobile device, and then applying variation or even a wholly different look for the desktop. We'll cover a few recipes on jQuery Mobile, a free and open source library of mobile UI elements and widgets. In addition, we'll build some client-side scripting to handle a unique look only for mobile devices.

Using the Safari Developer Tools' User Agent switcher

For developing mobile-first applications, you will need to deploy them locally and test the various features you have developed. Many of the responsive web recipes we have worked on so far relied on media queries to determine layout based on size to deliver the optimized view of your site. This is not the only way in which apps can deliver mobile layout, there are more. One method is, by sniffing the **user agent**.

You may already know about the user agent, but let's assume you don't. Besides, knowing everything already simply defeats the purpose of buying the book, now doesn't it? The user agent exists in the request header and identifies the client software making the request. It contains information about your processor, operating system version, browser, rendering engine, IP address, and other identifying information.

According to the needs of the project or the preference of the developer, some websites are designed to display different template files for mobile devices, or based on other details of the user agent data. This method requires a different server or client intelligence to read the user agent and interpret its data to deliver the presentation for that scenario.

So you've created a new web application, and the software displays the mobile template when the user agent details a mobile device. However, you want to be able to test it on the fly and not have to spin up a web server, so the next best thing is to use the user agent masking feature in Safari.

Using the Safari browser user agent switcher is a win-win, because not only does it mimic the user agent of the mobile Safari browser on iOS devices, but it also mimics the user agent of the Android browsers. So you can be at peace because the Android user agent was changed to say that it is also Mobile Safari, just to make your life easier. Wasn't that nice of them?

It's a good practice to clearly specify in your scope of work which browsers and user agents you will be testing for.

Getting ready

On an Apple computer, it's already installed. You are ahead of the game. So hang on while the Windows people catch up.

It looks unlikely that Apple will continue developing Safari for Windows. In fact, when you search for `Safari Windows`, the first link is not to the Safari homepage, but to an Apple support page with a link to the last Safari for Windows version, Safari 5.1.7 for Windows, not to the latest version (Version 6). But for the point of the recipe, let us continue.

How to do it...

First, open the Safari browser; you will want to go to a website that works as a demonstration for reading the user agent. Go to `http://whatsmyuseragent.com`, and the page will show you details of your user agent.

In Safari, go to **Safari | Preferences**, or press *Command* + *,*. In the **Advanced** tab, select the **Show Develop menu in menu bar** checkbox. You can see this illustrated in the following screenshot:

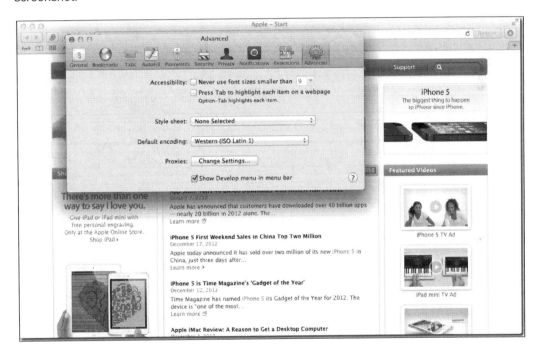

Now the menu bar shows the menu option **Develop**. Click on it and select **user agent**; a sub menu appears with different user agent options. There are a number of useful options here, but for this recipe, the most contextually useful ones are **Safari iOS 5.1 - iPhone** and **Safari iOS 5.1 - iPad** (it is very likely that you may have a version other than Version 5.1). This is demonstrated in the next screenshot:

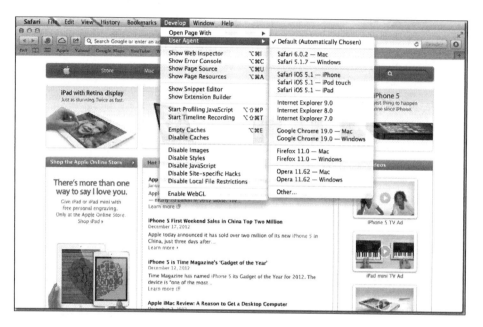

Select one of the iOS versions; the page will automatically be refreshed. You will now see the new user agent information, as illustrated in the following screenshot:

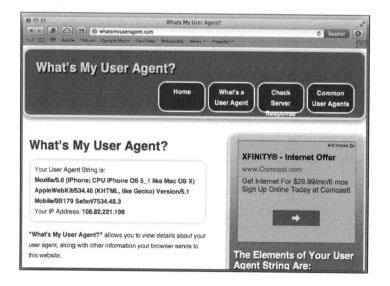

How it works...

I know it doesn't look like much happened, but what did happen was pretty big. The browser gave the server information about your computer and browser, and it served you a different web page as a result. You could build logic that delivers a special stylesheet, template, scripts, or completely different page content for mobile browsers.

Masking your user agent in Chrome with a plugin

The Chrome browser is rich with a multitude of plugins that you can use for just about any purpose under the sun. Let's explore a user-agent masking plugin to mask your user agent.

Why would you want to "mask" your user agent? Isn't that dishonest? Okay I'll admit it, it is. But here is one of the few cases where the ends genuinely justify the means. Besides, there's no harm done; it's not like the server figures out that your browser was lying to it and feels deceived and hurt. Masking your user agent gives you the power to convince the web server that your desktop browser is really a mobile browser. If the server believes you are using a mobile browser and its logic dictates that it should deliver a mobile version, then that's what you will get.

Getting ready

We want to find a way to be able to toggle between different user agents, and we want it to be really simple. In fact, we want it to be a button on the browser that we can press and switch. So where will we get this awesome bit of technological trickery? At the Chrome Web Store!

I've tried a few different Chrome browser plugins and have found one that has become a favorite in my responsive toolkit. The **User-Agent Switcher** for Chrome offers a snappy method to toggle between a comprehensive list of user agents. To get it, take the easier path and do a search for `Google UA Spoofer`.

How to do it...

The first search result should be a link to the User-Agent Switcher in the Chrome Web Store. If it is, go to it and click on the **ADD TO CHROME** button. That's all you need to do to install it. Using it will be easier.

Now look at the topmost section of your browser, to the right of the address bar, and find a new icon in the shape of a tiny mask. When you click on it, a menu of different browsers pops up, with submenus for available versions. We tested it, it is easy. See the following screenshot for proof:

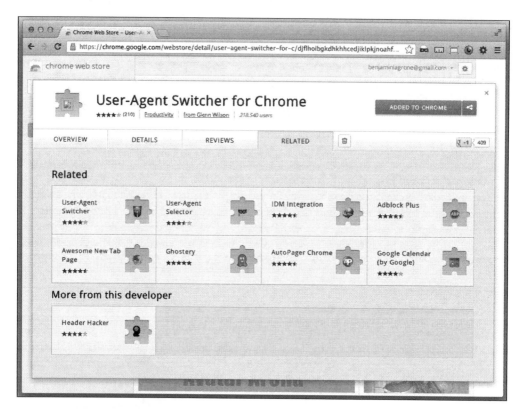

How it works...

The Chrome User Agent Spoofer browser plugin intercepts the normal browser user agent information in the request header and replaces it with the spoofed user agent information. So far, we've merely discussed how to test the user agent spoofer. How you will design your site to handle different user agents is a completely different subject.

To see it in action, go to `http://whatsmyuseragent.com/` and then toggle the browser plugin, from **iOS** to **iPhone**. You will see the user agent information change to **iPhone**. Try some more experiments and see how the masked user agent affects your favorite sites.

There's more...

Take a look at some of the various popular sites around the Web and you'll see how they handle different user agents. Some serve a different theme, while some redirect your browser to a subdomain for their mobile version. For example, `http://facebook.com` redirects to `http://m.facebook.com/?_rdr` for the iOS user agent, and `https://plus.google.com/` redirects to `https://plus.google.com/app/basic/stream` for a mobile version of their site.

The following screenshot shows how the masked user agent displays the page differently:

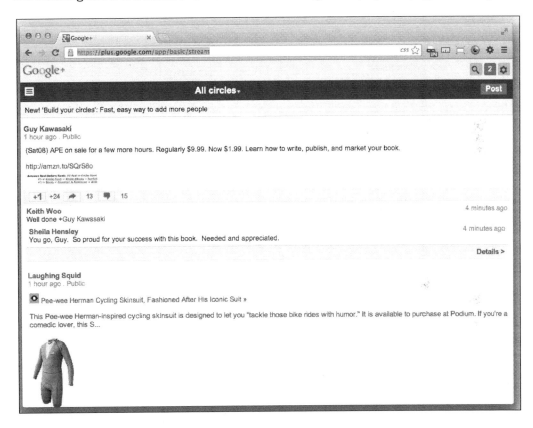

Using browser resizing plugins

I'll be frank with you; this recipe is about installing and using the browser resizing plugin that I use. If you have a better one, tell me about it. The one I have chosen after searching is called "Window Resizer".

Apart from testing on the target device, resizing the window with the plugin is the most accurate method of testing your media query. It is, however, only part of the testing you should put your responsive site through. Be sure to test it with emulators, and of course, actual devices, before deploying it. There's nothing worse than deploying a live site and watching it crash and burn after someone brings it to your attention.

Getting ready

Google is your friend. Search for `Window Resizer`. The first search result should be the Window Resizer plugin in the Chrome Web Store. There it is, like a beacon in the night! It has five stars, it's free; how could you not have clicked on that link already?

How to do it...

You will find yourself at the install page in the Chrome Web Store if you have gone along with me. You will see an attractive, wide, and calming deep blue button that says **+ ADD TO CHROME**. You are drawn to it and feel the need to click on it. You see in the blue, the sky at night that you look up to and wonder how far you will travel one day. You think about all the different sizes your browser could be. You think about the pain you feel while dragging the corners of your window, trying to guess its size. You can't take it anymore. Click on the button!

A flutter of movement across your browser window indicates that changes are being made. In the end, the blue button turns green. You are done here.

In your browser window, a new icon that looks like a tiny browser window has found its home on the right-hand side of your address field. Curiosity dictates that you need to know what this thing can do.

This is a virtually perfect way to test different media queries and responsive versions of your website, second only to testing it directly on the target device.

How it works...

Use the button to test your responsive designs to pixel-perfect precision. When you click on it, it unveils a list of different browser window sizes. Each one is perfectly measured and will bend your browser's size according to your will. The browser plugin does all of the guesswork and precise measuring for you, as it directly affects the browser window size at the click of a button! See the following screenshot:

Learning the viewport and its options

If nothing else, it can be said that the purpose of the viewport is to tame the mobile browser window. The viewport is vital to determining how your mobile browser renders the mobile web page.

Getting ready

If you are using an Apple computer, an iOS simulator can be obtained by downloading Xcode from Apple. It is part of the Xcode package. I usually get to it by using Spotlight. Press *Command* + the Space bar; the Spotlight search field appears in the top-right corner of your screen. Start typing in `iOS Simulator`, and it will appear in the search results. Click on it to spin up the iOS simulator.

How to do it...

Open up one of the responsive projects that you've done from a previous recipe project. I suggest opening up the `resp-width-layout-media-query.html` project from the *Creating a responsive width layout with media query* recipe.

To get an iOS simulator for Windows, you'll need to find one on the Web. After searching, I found a good one at `http://iphone4simulator.com/`, and another at `http://iphonetester.com/`. To use them, you'll need to upload your project files to a web host before this web simulator can view it. The simulator cannot read files from your local hard drive, unless you are running a local web server.

First, for comparison, view the file in your browser. Then in your iPhone simulator, enter the URL of the files, and you'll discover the shock and horror of seeing your site looking just like the desktop version. I experienced the same frustration when my early responsive projects did not work the way I wanted them to. The problem is that the mobile browser does not know what size you want it to be. It is smart but not clever. Like all software, it needs good instructions. So take a deep breath and we will fix it together. The problem is illustrated in the following screenshot:

You can tell the mobile browser what it should do by configuring the viewport. First add the simple viewport `<meta>` tag:

```
<meta name="viewport">
```

Before we go any further, I should tell you about this caveat. If you don't intend to do a design for the mobile device, then leave out the viewport `<meta>` tag. It can cause unintended consequences on your page delivery. In fact, it might just show a sliver of your page and not allow the viewer to pan out our scroll to view the whole page.

Now we will discuss its options. First, the width; I'm a big fan of the K.I.S.S. principle (keep it short and simple). Unless you have a reason for specifying a particular width, enter the device width as the viewport width. This way, it will read the device width and set that as the page width. Setting a specific width, `1000px` for example, will look okay on your iPad, but on your phone devices it will render too wide and nullify the media queries smaller than that width.

```
<meta name="viewport" content="width=device-width">
```

Once you've made the change, open your iOS simulator's browser and view the file. You can see the fixed version in the following screenshot:

Next, let's talk about scaling. Let's assume you have no special request to do anything weird, like starting the scale with any value other than one. Add to the viewport `<meta>` tag, the initial scale value of `1`.

Okay, I know I said don't do anything weird, but just for demonstration, change your initial scale to `2`. Refresh your screen.

Next, change it to `0.4`. Remember this is just for demonstration. Please refresh your screen again. In the portrait view, you can see that the web page uses the small screen media query. Now, change the orientation of the simulator to bring it to landscape mode. You will now see that the larger media query is active. That was an interesting experiment; now change your initial scale back to `1`.

Finally, do you want your viewers to be able to zoom in and out using the multi-touch pinch? Use the meta attribute `maximum-scale` to limit how much zooming you want to allow. Set the maximum scale to `1` if you want to disallow zooming.

```
maximum-scale=1
```

How it works...

The viewport `<meta>` tag was included in the Safari Mobile browser by Apple initially, and was then added to other browsers. It is used to define the width the page should be read in. When the browser sees the viewport `<meta>` tag with the width attribute defined, it loads the page at the scale defined in that width setting, coupled with the initial scale attribute.

Adding tags for jQuery Mobile

This recipe jumps deep into a new area of responsive design, that is, mobile-first. Mobile-first, in a nutshell, means that you would first design for a mobile version of the site and then make modifications for the desktop. Now, this does not mean that you are designing a "mobile only" website, only that designing your layouts and styles for mobile comes first.

Mobile-first may require rethinking your designs, or at least designing from a different perspective. But isn't change good? Can't we all improve our design skills by trying out new approaches? Isn't Darwinism merely the survival of those who are best suited to adapt to change?

So let's go ahead with an open mind and try some mobile-first development.

Getting ready

First, hop on over to the jQuery Mobile site. It is at `http://jquerymobile.com`. Otherwise, you can simply search for `jQuery Mobile` if you are lazy like me. I'll provide the direct link if you don't want to search for it and because you are my special buddy. The direct link to the site is `http://lmgtfy.com/?q=jquery+mobile&l=1`. I'll even shorten that for you; go to `http://bit.ly/TMpuB8`.

Here, you can download the library if you want to host your files locally (and there are some very good reasons to do that); for this recipe, however, we can do it the more expedient way and let someone else host all the necessary files.

The jQuery Mobile site has a veritable cornucopia of docs and samples. It even has download builders, so you can scale down the necessary libraries to just those that are needed to run your mobile web app.

How to do it...

First, create a new HTML document in your IDE. Add the viewport `<meta>` tag to your header:

```
<meta name="viewport" content="width=device-width, initial-scale=1">
```

Next, include links to the jQuery Mobile CSS and JavaScript files.

```
<link rel="stylesheet" href="http://code.jquery.com/mobile/1.2.0/
jquery.mobile-1.2.0.min.css" />
<script src="http://code.jquery.com/jquery-1.8.2.min.js"></script>
<script src="http://code.jquery.com/mobile/1.2.0/jquery.mobile-
1.2.0.min.js"></script>
```

It's worth it to pause for a pedagogical minute and talk about your stylesheets. In the previous piece of code, we are linking to a remote jQuery CSS. I would recommend you (if you are going to host this file locally) to leave it as is and add all of your new CSS for your elements in an entirely different stylesheet. Additionally, if you want to make any changes to jQuery's CSS, add another CSS file and make explicit namespaced overrides, or use the `!important` override. Name this something like `jQuery-mobile-changes.css`. I don't expect that you will need to do this, but just in case you do, this is a good way to handle it. I recommend this because when a new version of jQuery is released, you won't need to break your site when you upgrade.

That covers most of your header. Now let's create some basic content for the page. First, let's wrap the page with a `<div>` element:

```
<body>
    <div>

    </div>
</body>
```

One of the really great features of jQuery Mobile is that it uses tags, which you can put inside the HTML elements that are not used to render your page. The benefit is that you can use the same template for your desktop site just by swapping out the jQuery Mobile scripts and styles for your own. Next, add some tags to your wrapping `<div>` element that tell jQuery Mobile to act on this page. Add `data-role="page"` to the element.

```
<div data-role="page">
```

Let's demonstrate by building a sample text page.

Add a new `h1` header title wrapped in a `<div>` element. To the `<div>` element, add a `data-role="header"` attribute. Then, open the file in a browser to see the jQuery Mobile theme.

```
<div data-role="header">
    <h1>Adding tags for jQuery Mobile</h1>
</div>
```

That's a good start; let's continue by adding some more examples of page structure in jQuery Mobile.

 You can also give these elements IDs and classes for your desktop version.

Next, add a body. Add a paragraph of some filler text and then wrap the paragraph in a `<div>` element. Assign an HTML5 data attribute `data-role:"content"` to the `<div>` element.

```
<div data-role="content">
  <p>
    Lorem ipsum dolor sit amet, consectetuer adipiscing elit. Aenean
commodo ligula eget dolor. Aenean massa....
  </p>
</div>
```

Similarly, add a footer. Wrap a simple text in an `h4` tag, and wrap that in a `<div>` element. Now give that `<div>` element the attribute `data-role="footer"`:

```
<div data-role="footer">
  <h4>The Footer</h4>
</div>
```

That's all there is to it. The jQuery Mobile site has great documentation and examples on how to further build mobile sites using their framework. We will be going through more jQuery Mobile recipes in this chapter. Go check them out. This is how your page will look with jQuery Mobile:

How it works...

jQuery Mobile uses HTML5 data attributes to fire the scripts for markup and widgets. The script will automatically act when you place the data attribute in the element.

Adding a second page in jQuery Mobile

There is a really cool feature in jQuery Mobile that allows you to divide a bigger HTML page into smaller, digestible parts. Imagine you have a page that has a lot of content and you don't want to force your audience to keep scrolling down to read. Consider using jQuery Mobile's multipage template structure. The user experience of a web page on a mobile device is very different from that of the one on a desktop. On the old desktop Web, it was often said, "Content is king"; now that the Web is mobile, there is limited space, and it's easy for all that content to become too much content. You may want to consider limiting some of what is displayed on each page. In this recipe, we will use jQuery Mobile to divide a large page with lots of data into smaller digestible bits.

Getting ready

In the previous recipe, we built a simple page using jQuery Mobile tags. Let's dig up the file from that recipe and save it as a new file to work on. This will serve as a starting point for this recipe.

How to do it...

Add an ID of `p1` to the outer, wrapping `<div>` element (with the page `data-role`). This will help jQuery identify and transition between the multipage elements.

```
<div data-role="page" id="p1">
```

You have created what jQuery Mobile will recognize as the first page among the multiple pages. Let's create the next one. Create new opening and closing `<div>` elements right before the closing `<body>` tag. Give this `<div>` element a `data-role="page"` element just like the previous instance, and an ID of `p2`.

```
<div data-role="page" id="p2">
```

This page will need `data-role="header"`, `data-role="content"`, and `data-role="footer"`, just like the previous `<div>` element `data-role="page"`. You can also simply copy the previous section and paste it into the `"p2"` `<div>` element.

```
<div data-role="page" id="p2">
  <div data-role="header">
    <h1>The second page</h1>
  </div>
  <div data-role="content">
    <p> Lorem ipsum dolor sit amet...</p>
  </div>
  <div data-role="footer">
    <h4>The Footer</h4>
  </div>
</div>
```

We are almost done; we only need to link the pages together. In the `"p1"` content, right before the closing `<div>` element, add an `href` anchor tag linking to `"#p2"`:

```
<a href="#p2">Page 2</a>
```

In the `"p2"` `<div>` element, inside the `data-role="content"` `<div>` element, add another link, linking back to the first page ID:

```
<a href="#p1">Back to Page 1</a>
```

Now save the file and launch it. You'll see it create a nice and native-looking mobile website. Click on the **Page** links and you'll see that there is a smooth fade transition between the multipage pages. You will also notice that the back button works as well. If you think about it, this behavior is very useful for the native app look and feel of our website. See the first page in the next screenshot:

The second page is illustrated in the following screenshot:

How it works...

jQuery Mobile can load multiple pages within a single HTML page and present them as multiple pages or subpages. To link between them, simply add `HREF="#page"`. When that link is clicked, jQuery Mobile will look for an internal page with that ID and smoothly write it to the viewport.

Making a list element in jQuery Mobile

Let me be the first to say this: I love unordered lists. Conversely, I have an equally intense aversion to "programmer art" tables. In fact, I've earned a reputation with the people I work with as a "destroyer of tables". There are very few sets of things in HTML that can't be displayed using a good list, which is why I adore the way in which jQuery Mobile handles lists. jQuery Mobile lists, in my opinion, prove why a list is the superior way to present data, menus, navigation, and so on. Enough of my abnormal obsession with unordered lists, let's go through a recipe about jQuery Mobile lists together.

Getting ready

Think about how many awful tables you have put out on the Internet and what terrible things all of that deadweight code has turned into. That's enough admonishment for the crimes of your past, let's move forward and make some jQuery Mobile lists!

How to do it...

Create a new page with the necessary header information that jQuery Mobile wants. Include the viewport `<meta>` tag and the links to the jQuery Mobile stylesheet, the jQuery JavaScript, and finally, the jQuery Mobile JavaScript. You can host these locally on your own server or use those hosted at `http://code.jquery.com`.

```
<meta name="viewport" content="width=device-width, initial-scale=1">
<link rel="stylesheet" href="http://code.jquery.com/mobile/1.3.0-
beta.1/jquery.mobile-1.3.0-beta.1.min.css" />
<script src="http://code.jquery.com/jquery-1.9.min.js"></script>
<script src="http://code.jquery.com/mobile/1.3.0-beta.1/jquery.mobile-
1.3.0-beta.1.min.js"></script>
```

Next create a `<div>` element with the `data-role="page"` attribute. This is an HTML5 attribute that jQuery Mobile uses to deploy style, elements, and widgets.

```
<div data-role="page"></div>
```

Inside that `<div>` wrap, create an unordered list of your favorite robots.

```
<ul>
    <li>Hero 1</li>
    <li>Bender</li>
    <li>Optimus Prime</li>
    <li>Soundwave</li>
    <li>Wall-E</li>
    <li>Maximillian</li>
    <li>R2-D2</li>
    <li>GORT</li>
    <li>Cat Quadcopter</li>
    <li>Robocop</li>
    <li>The Maschinenmensch</li>
</ul>
```

Let's not launch this right now. We both already know that this will look like a plain old list. If you were making a separate CSS for a desktop version, you could style this list there.

Add the attribute `data-role="listview"` to your unordered list. Now you can launch this and see that it looks like a styled list of robots.

Let's keep going. Because this is a list, and we love lists, we're going to just keep playing with it and see what jQuery Mobile can do with it. Add another attribute, `data-inset="true"`. Now your list has a cool wrap border around it so each item does not stretch to the edge of the screen.

Sometimes, you may end up with a really long list, like when you make a list of cool robots, because robots are cool, and you don't want to have to keep scrolling and scrolling to select your favorite robot. jQuery Mobile has a built-in solution for this, a filtering element. Invoke it by adding a new attribute, `data-filter="true"`. Refresh your mobile browser; you will see an input at the top to enter a `filtertext` element. The Search widget uses a client-side search/filter to filter out list items. No longer will you have to scroll down to find that awesome robot at the bottom of your list.

Let's take this to the next level. What if we want to be able to filter the robots by some other data that we don't want to display, such as the robot manufacturer? You can add the attribute `data-filtertext=""` to each list item. It would look something like this:

```
<li data-filtertext="Mom's Robots"><a href="#">Bender</a></li>
<li data-filtertext="Hasbro"><a href="#">Optimus Prime</a></li>
```

See the following figure for a demonstration:

This list can even be styled differently by assigning a theme in the data attribute. Try adding `data-theme="a"` to the unordered list. Now try using the letters b through f. Each one has a different theme that you can apply to the list.

Here is the unordered list with the different attributes we have used so far. The figure after the following piece of code shows the different themes in action.

```
<ul data-role="listview" data-inset="true" data-filter="true" data-theme="g">
```

Next let's see what happens when these list items become links. Add an `href` anchor tag to each item.

```
<li><a href="#">Bender</a></li>
```

When you refresh your screen, you will see how it adds the icon to indicate that it is a clickable link. However, since `href` links to #, it does not load a new page. See the following screenshot for the illustrated example:

Let's break this list apart, into two groups, the "destroy all humans" group and the "workerbot" group. Add another list item for the first group to the top of the list, with the attribute `data-role="list-divider"`.

```
<li data-role="list-divider">destroy all humans</li>
```

Add another similar list item about halfway down the list.

```
<li data-role="list-divider">workerbot</li>
```

This is shown in the next screenshot:

You might feel the need to organize your robots into these groups if it makes you feel good. We can take this impulse further and make the lists nested. Add a `ul` element to the `list-divider` that you just made, and then cut and paste the first half of the robots' `li` code into this `ul` element.

```
<li data-role="list-divider">destroy all humans
  <ul>
    <li><a href="#">Bender</a></li>
    <li><a href="#">Optimus Prime</a></li>
    <li><a href="#">Soundwave</a></li>
    <li><a href="#">Wall-E</a></li>
    <li><a href="#">Maximillian</a></li>
  </ul>
</li>
```

Do the same for the next list section. Then, refresh to see the new results. Check out the following figure:

You can add an h3 header title wrap to the parent list items, and even a description wrapped in a paragraph element. These lists keep getting fancier and fancier.
See the following screenshot:

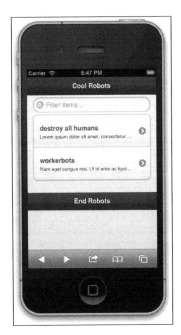

So let's do one final list feature and call it a recipe. This is a gorgeous widget for handling lists. You can make a list of collapsible list elements. We're going to change the `ul` and `li` list item attributes. First, make the outer `ul` list element contain the attributes `data-role="collapsible-set"`, `data-theme="b"`, and `data-content-theme="d"`.

```
<ul data-role="collapsible-set" data-theme="b" data-content-theme="d">
```

Each of the two direct child `li` elements of that `ul` element should have the attribute `data-role="collapsible"`.

```
<li data-role="collapsible"><h2>workerbots</h2><p>...<p>
```

Give the attributes `data-role="listview"` and `data-filter="true"` to the child `ul` element of that collapsible `li` list item.

```
<ul data-role="listview" data-filter="true">
```

The whole unordered list list will look like this:

```
<ul data-role="collapsible-set" data-theme="b" data-content-theme="d">
  <li data-role="collapsible">
    <h2>destroy all humans</h2>
    <p>Lorem ipsum dolor sit amet, consectetur adipiscing elit.
Integer consectetur quam in nulla malesuada congue volutpat mi
molestie. Quisque faucibus, nisi ut malesuada volutpat</p>
    <ul data-role="listview" data-filter="true">
      <li><a href="#">Bender</a></li>
      <li><a href="#">Optimus Prime</a></li>
      <li><a href="#">Soundwave</a></li>
      <li><a href="#">Wall-E</a></li>
      <li><a href="#">Maximillian</a></li>
    </ul>
  </li>
  <li data-role="collapsible" >
    <h3>workerbots</h3>
    <p>Nam eget congue nisi. Ut id ante ac ligula congue auctor a et
lacus. Suspendisse varius sem sed elit tincidunt convallis.</p>
    <ul data-role="listview" data-filter="true">
      <li><a href="#">R2-D2</a></li>
      <li><a href="#">GORT</a></li>
      <li><a href="#">Cat Quadcopter</a></li>
      <li><a href="#">Robocop</a></li>
      <li><a href="#">The Maschinenmensch</a></li>
    </ul>
  </li>
</ul>
```

The finished list has been depicted in the following figure:

How it works...

That was amazing. You did not have to do much apart from making a good list. No table could have pulled that off, ever. As long as you use the HTML5 data attributes in your elements, jQuery Mobile will do the heavy lifting and turn your list into a sleek, native-looking web app. jQuery Mobile takes the data attribute (which doesn't affect the layout or style), and from it, it rewrites the HTML and CSS for the mobile version.

Adding a mobile, native-looking button with jQuery Mobile

Let's make buttons! Making a button may seem like a very trivial part of the design, but contrarily, when you are building a web application, a button can be a very important part of the site's usability.

jQuery Mobile has an impressive array of button invocations, and they are all easy to use. They are usable within many other jQuery Mobile widgets as well. In addition, it is just as easy to make a button from a link as it is to make one from a `form input` element.

Getting ready

In your IDE or text editor, spin up a new HTML document and add the requisite header tags. First add the viewport `<meta>` tag, followed by links to the jQuery Mobile CSS and the JavaScript libraries jQuery and jQuery Mobile.

```
<meta name="viewport" content="width=device-width, initial-scale=1">
<link rel="stylesheet" href="http://code.jquery.com/mobile/1.2.0/
jquery.mobile-1.2.0.min.css" />
<script src="http://code.jquery.com/jquery-1.8.2.min.js"></script>
<script src="http://code.jquery.com/mobile/1.2.0/jquery.mobile-
1.2.0.min.js"></script>
```

In your HTML `<body>` tag, add a `<div>` element with the HTML5 attribute `data-role="page"`. Inside it, add an h1 header and wrap it with a `<div>` element with the `data-role="header"` attribute. Following the header element, add a `<div>` element with the `data-role="content"` attribute. See the following code snippet:

```
<div data-role="page">
  <div data-role="header"><h1>There be buttons</h1></div>
  <div data-role="content">...</div>
</div>
```

How to do it...

Let's compare some different methods to create a basic button. First, there is the HTML5 element `<button>`, various `<input>` form elements `button` and `submit`, and an `href` pseudo button. Put one of each inside your content `<div>` element.

```
<button>HTML5 Button</button>

<input type="button" value="Input Button" />

<input type="submit" value="Submit Button" />

<a href="#" data-role="button">Link button</a>
```

Launch your new page. You will see four new buttons that look identical (with the exception of the text). You can see that each of these methods is delivered the same way. This is impressive, as your non-mobile version of the template file may require you to use a certain type of `submit` element (which is not exactly mobile-first, but no one is perfect). See the following screenshot:

Let's continue with this recipe now by demonstrating how to add icons to the buttons using jQuery Mobile. This is a simple, one-step process; it uses an HTML5 data attribute, the `data-icon` attribute. In your first button, add the `data-icon="delete"` attribute; in the next one, add the `data-icon="check"` attribute; add `data-icon="plus"` to the next one; and finally, add `data-icon="arrow-l"` to the last button in this set of buttons. There is a list of icons that you can put in there; you can find them in the documentation.

```
<button data-icon="delete">HTML5 Button</button>

<input type="button" value="Input Button" data-icon="check" />

<input type="submit" value="Submit Button" data-icon="plus"/>

<a href="#" data-role="button" data-icon="arrow-l">Link button</a>
```

The following screenshot shows the new buttons:

You can also make a button smaller by adding the `data-mini="true"` attribute and position the icon at the right, left, top, or bottom corners of the button using the `data-iconpos` attribute. Otherwise, you can use the `data-iconpos="notext"` attribute to only show the icon. See the following screenshot:

The default behavior for these jQuery Mobile buttons is to stretch across the whole screen. You can change this by adding the attribute `data-inline="true"`.

```
<button data-icon="delete" data-mini="true" data-inline="true">HTML5
Button</button>

<input type="button" value="Input Button" data-icon="check" data-
iconpos="right" data-inline="true"/>

<input type="submit" value="Submit Button" data-icon="plus" data-
iconpos="top" data-inline="true"/>

<a href="#" data-role="button" data-icon="arrow-l" data-
iconpos="notext" data-inline="true">Link button</a>
```

It's messy, but you can see it in action here:

They will become inline elements, similar to the list items that are displayed as inline. We're almost done, but there's still some fun to be had. We can also make button groups easily. Remove the `data-inline="true"` attribute that you added in the previous section. Next, wrap the button elements with a `<div>` element, with the attribute `data-role="controlgroup"`.

```
<div data-role="controlgroup">

    <button data-icon="delete" data-mini="true" >HTML5 Button</button>
```

```
    <input type="button" value="Input Button" data-icon="check" data-
    iconpos="right"/>

    <input type="submit" value="Submit Button" data-icon="plus" data-
    iconpos="top" />

    <a href="#" data-role="button" data-icon="arrow-l" data-
    iconpos="notext" >Link button</a>

</div>
```

Now you can see the potential for creative button groups and keeping them together in a pretty package. Let's add some more effects to the button group. If you add `data-type="horizontal"` to the `"controlgroup"` `<div>` element, you'll make a mess that you'll need to clean up. One way to clean this up would be to change all of the `data-iconpos` attributes to `"notext"`.

Finally, as we have seen in the previous jQuery Mobile recipes, the `data-theme` attribute can make your buttons colorful. To quickly show this effect, add a different `data-theme` attribute (a, b, c, e) to each of the buttons (I skipped d, it looked too much like c). These are illustrated in the next screenshot:

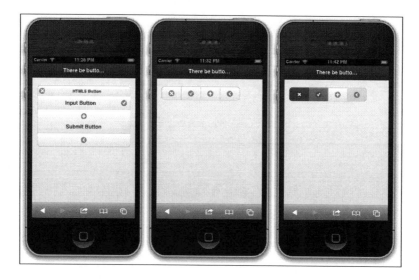

How it works...

All you really need to know about how this works is which data tags to use to make jQuery Mobile pick up the HTML elements and turn them into mobile-native buttons. It happens auto-magically actually, when you have the correct attributes, and it works no matter what method of the `submit` button it is applied to. jQuery Mobile fires an event on the HTML5 attributes and adds the HTML and styles to the rendered page.

Adding a mobile stylesheet for mobile browsers only using the media query

In this recipe, we want to be able to use a stylesheet in the template only for use by mobile browsers. JavaScript aside, there is no way in client-side rendering to listen for the user agent and deliver some logic or special template for mobile browsers. Let's take the K.I.S.S. approach and get as close as we can with a media query.

Of course, there are numerous ways to write JavaScript to detect a user agent, and we will cover that in a later recipe, but for now let's write a killer media query to lock down the mobile browser for a specific CSS. In the previous recipes, our media queries were performed inside a stylesheet. This one will be different as we will put it inside the HTML header link. Change is good, do not worry. The reason we are putting the media query within the HTML link to the CSS file is that we want to call that CSS file only under special circumstances. This recipe is especially useful when you are using mobile-first design and technologies like jQuery Mobile.

Getting ready

Fire up your handy IDE and start a new HTML page. Be sure to add your viewport `<meta>` tag. If you like, you can add a paragraph of text in the HTML body.

How to do it...

In the `<body>` tag of your new HTML file, add two paragraphs of text. Each with a different class (class="a" and class="b"). This will be enough HTML to demonstrate the media query at work.

```
<p class="a">Lorem ipsum dolor sit amet, consectetur adipiscing
elit.</p>
<p class="b">Nulla ante tortor, rutrum eu sollicitudin eget, vehicula
quis sem. Nullam cursus placerat luctus.</p>
```

Now back to the `<head>` tag. First, let's add the viewport `<meta>` tag. Include the content attribute "width=device-width". Next, add some simple style for the font (font-size: 100%).

```
<style>
  html{font-size:100%}
</style>
```

Next we're going to add the link to the mobile CSS stylesheet with a media query. The basic stylesheet link contains `rel="stylesheet"` and the path. Add to it the conditions it needs to satisfy to use that stylesheet. Add a media query for `screen` and `max-device-width=320px`. Your CSS link should look like this:

```
<link rel="stylesheet" media="screen and (max-device-width:320px)"
href="mobile.css" />
```

There's nothing more for us to do in the HTML file, so create a CSS file in the same directory and name it `mobile.css`. Open it to edit it. We don't need to do much here, only one line is sufficient. Add a line for the `b` class paragraph and give it an attribute of `2rem` for the font size. REM means Relative EM, or relative to the root font size (in case you skipped the responsive typography recipes).

```
p.b{font-size:2rem}
```

Now let's try it out. Open your HTML file in a browser, and then open it in your mobile device simulator. Here, you can see the mobile device has a unique presentation with a different font size for the `b` class paragraph. See this recipe illustrated in the following screenshot:

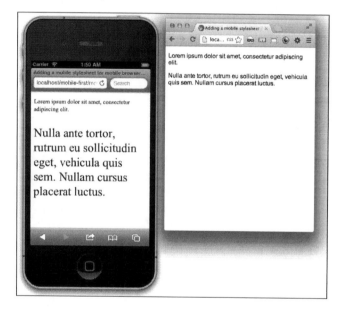

How it works...

The media query is designed to become active only on devices that have a screen resolution of 320px or lesser. Anything greater than that ignores (it still does get downloaded) the CSS file linked. You could additionally write media queries for other specific devices as well.

Adding JavaScript for mobile browsers only

In the previous recipe, we wrote a media query inside a stylesheet link. This was useful for our own mobile-first responsive web development. However, when using JavaScript code specifically for mobile platforms, such as jQuery Mobile, you might not want to have them initiated on desktop computers. Let's build a tiny JavaScript code that detects the mobile device screen size and then deploys jQuery Mobile for it but not for the desktop.

Getting ready

Mobile-first technologies like jQuery Mobile are amazing tools when you have a server-side technology. They do need server-side logic to work the best. If you are not fortunate enough to have access to server-side logic, you can employ some client-side tricks to work your magic.

How to do it...

If you have not looked through the jQuery Mobile recipes, take a look now; we're going to reuse one of the recipes that we have used already.

Open up one of the files that you created in the previous recipe using jQuery Mobile. You can use the *Adding a mobile, native-looking button with jQuery Mobile* recipe. If you worked through this recipe on making a mobile, native-looking button, use it to follow along.

When we last saw this file, the jQuery Mobile script took your plain old boring HTML buttons and turned them into cool jQuery Mobile buttons. All you needed was to include the HTML5 data attributes in your elements, and jQuery Mobile did the rest auto-magically. So what if you only want this to happen on a mobile device?

Well, you would be in trouble if it weren't for the magic of client-side scripting. We first want the script to be aware that it is dealing with a mobile device. One way is by querying the user agent of the DOM element. I've seen a few people do that, but it's complicated enough to be bug-prone. So instead, let's detect the size of the device screen. Most mobile viewports are at most 600 pixels wide or smaller; so for now, you are safe if you are developing applications assuming that that is the correct maximum size.

So let's make the script get the screen width from the DOM; if it's smaller than 600px, go get jQuery Mobile script. First, using jQuery, fire a function when the document loads.

```
$(document).ready(function(){
  //
});
```

Inside the function, write a conditional statement; if the screen is smaller than 600, then do something.

```
$(document).ready(function(){
  if (window.screen.width < 600){
    //Do something!
  };
});
```

That's a good start, but let's be more specific about "doing something". What we want the script to do is fetch and run the jQuery Mobile script. A good method for that is jQuery's $.getScript() function. So put that in the if condition, including the jQuery Mobile source URL.

```
$(document).ready(function(){
  if (window.screen.width < 600){
    $.getScript("http://code.jquery.com/mobile/1.2.0/jquery.mobile-
1.2.0.min.js");
  };
});
```

Now load the page in your mobile device emulator.

How it works...

If the emulator successfully spoofs the device width in the request, you will see the jQuery Mobile version of the HTML page. In your desktop browser, no matter what size your browser window is, you will not be able to load the jQuery Mobile script.

jQuery's $.getScript() is a function that loads an external script into the header. You can use it like we did in the recipe, to conditionally load an external JavaScript and additionally execute functions on its successful loading.

6
Optimizing Responsive Content

In this chapter, you will learn about:

▸ Responsive testing using IE's Developer Tools

▸ Browser testing – using plugins

▸ Development environments – getting a free IDE

▸ Virtualization – downloading VirtualBox

▸ Getting a browser resizer for Chrome

Introduction

The recipes in this chapter cover a broad range of topics. There is no code covered in this chapter, but the recipes fall under a more functional umbrella. This chapter talks more about the tools you will use to develop and test code. Here we will make sure that our code works the way we want it to. While this topic may seem uninteresting, it is as important as honing your skills in design and development. No amount of confident boasting makes a frontend developer immune to errors, and there are simply too many things that can go wrong as a project grows. Please go through these recipes and try out the tools, they will make your work easier and less prone to errors down the line.

Responsive testing using IE's Developer Tools

Having a responsive design also includes having an optimized design for all of the prolific browsers, which is without equivocation, the least exciting aspect of Responsive Design. There is no way to sugarcoat this, many features of HTML5 and CSS3 are not supported even in the future versions of Internet Explorer, and those that are supported can sometimes be rendered incorrectly. To add more madness, Versions 7, 8, and 9 all behave differently, and there are countless users who just cannot or will not update their browsers. There's also the problem of a number of companies having invested in web software that only runs on older versions of Internet Explorer. This lack of updating has been solved by other browsers such as Chrome and Firefox; the Internet Explorer team really needs to catch up. However, because you want your work to always look good no matter what browser it's in, the responsibility is yours to make it work for every browser.

Getting ready

Talk to your clients and fellow designers on the project about what levels of support you want to provide for Internet Explorer users. There are a few strategies possible for supporting the older versions of Internet Explorer. Talk about how much additional work each will require to support older versions of Internet Explorer, how much it should cost, and who should pay for it. The last thing you want is to launch your clients' brand new web project and them starting to complain that it looks broken in their favorite, degraded old browser.

The first question to ask is: what can you do with Internet Explorer F12 Developer Tools? The answer is, you can use it to debug the rather wonkish way in which Internet Explorer is displaying your code, and to toggle between the different versions of Internet Explorer to see how your site looks in each.

How to do it...

If you don't use a Windows computer, you won't be able to natively get a hold of Internet Explorer F12 Developer Tools. That doesn't mean that you simply forget about testing for IE and hope what you do works. There are legions of web pages and plugins that promise to accurately emulate the quirks of IE's multitude of versions. I have tried many and found that there was not one that actually stood up to testing against the original IE Developer Tools. So after much trial and failure, I found that the only dependable way to test for IE, without having to go and buy several computers just for testing, was to use virtualization. I have a few instances of Windows on virtual machines, with different versions of Internet Explorer installed. I have found that it's the only way to be sure. If you want to learn how to get started with virtualization, see the *Virtualization – Downloading VirtualBox* recipe in this chapter.

So once we have started up our Windows machine and updated to the latest version of Internet Explorer, let us see what the F12 Developer Tools can do for us. Either press *F12* on your keyboard or click on the gear icon on the toolbar at the top-right corner of the screen to display the F12 Developer Tools. This is demonstrated in the following screenshot:

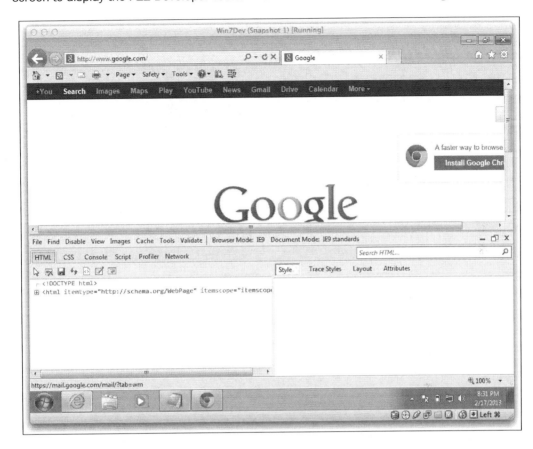

The first useful thing you can do here is click on the pointer icon and move your mouse over the browser window to the element that is misbehaving. While the mouse is traveling, you will see that the element your mouse is moving over gets a white border around it. Once you see the white border around the element you want to inspect, click on it; the HTML pane will then bring that line of HTML code into focus in the left-hand side window, and its CSS on the right. In the CSS pane, you can edit the tree of CSS attributes for each element.

If you want to add a CSS attribute, click on the **Attributes** button. By scrolling down to the bottom of the page, you can add a new name and value pair for the attributes. You can use these two tools to test out different CSS attribute variations or debug some strange IE behavior.

The other useful tool is the **Browser Mode** select menu. You can use this tool to toggle between the different browser versions. This is a good tool to do on-the-fly checking of your work. Here, you can also test out your IE-specific stylesheets. You can see this in following screenshot:

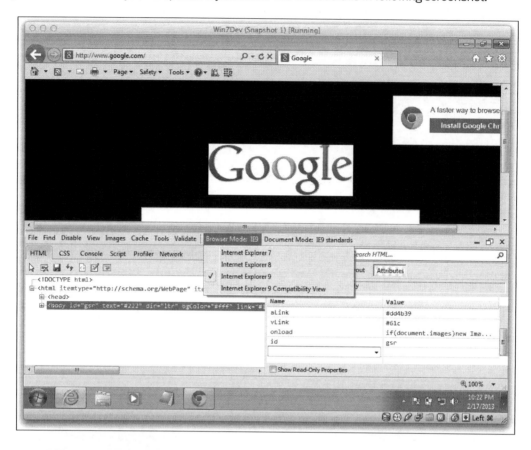

How it works...

According to MSDN, the F12 Developer Tools represents the actual way in which the Document Object Model (DOM) interprets the page, and not the code you actually wrote.

There's more...

An additional pitfall you may fall into occurs when you are designing a site that may be accessed as internal software or on the same domain as the intranet. Internet Explorer will use Internet Explorer 7 Compatibility View as the default rendering view.

Compatibility mode was a feature added in IE 8 so that websites that were developed for the older standards could still work in the new browsers. Often, people's browsers are set to render intranet sites in compatibility mode. To make a site that is built for IE 7 work in the most recent Internet Explorer, you would have to set this `<meta>` tag to render it at the desired rendering version. To force the browser to always render this using the most recent rendering engine, you'll need to specify the following `<meta>` tag to prevent this.

```
<meta http-equiv="X-UA-Compatible" content="IE=edge,chrome=1">
```

Browser testing – using plugins

Testing is a big deal in any and all development processes. For some, the idea of testing is incorrectly perceived as a sign of poor workmanship or criticality of their work. This idea could not be more wrong. On the contrary, rigorous and thorough testing is the only way to ensure that your software approaches a state of perfection. I consider myself very fortunate to work with QA testers whose role is to test the work of the development team. Having had to do all of my own testing (in a previous life), I can say that this is a luxury.

In this recipe, we will discuss a specific area of testing, cross-browser testing. Not too long ago, this was less complicated, and more challenging at the same time. The idea of testing a web project for mobile devices was not very common; it was simply not expected to look remotely similar, or even display the same content. Therefore the number of devices you needed to test for were usually limited to what you could spin up in a virtual environment, and they were all desktop devices. The tools were also limited, and were often only virtual desktops with older browser versions. Remember those stubborn people who refused to move beyond IE6?

One approach to browser testing is to simply get your credit card out and buy every device you think it would be plausible for your software to be viewed on. I have never actually met anyone who has done this, but I think one or two of the fairy tales I read to my children spoke of this sort of phenomenon happening. This is not a practical solution for people who work for money. This has resulted in a market of paid and free cross-browser testing tools popping up on the Internet.

Getting ready

If you were starting to think that this is going to be an expensive recipe, calm down. There will be no need to go out and buy every new mobile device on the market. There are plenty of emulators that will cover most of your bases.

How to do it...

I have scoured the Internet and built a list of free tools for you to use for testing. Go through the list with me and check them out. Open one of your previous responsive web design (RWD) recipe project files in a browser tab to continue. For each of the simulators, you will have to open the file by entering it into the simulated browser's address bar. If you have not done any of these or simply do not have the files handy, go to the Packt website and download them. On to the simulators.

First let's look at online browser simulators. Go to `http://theleggett.com/tools/webapptester`. Here you can test you RWD site on a web simulation of iOS devices. It can read your localhost files. You can toggle between the portrait and landscape modes and choose iPhone versus iPad. It's simple enough and you don't need to install any complicated applications or plugins. This is good if you need something in a pinch, want to test fast, and don't want to install anything. You can see the simulator in action in the following screenshot:

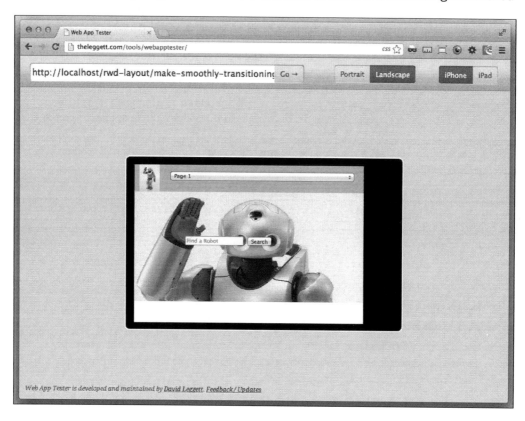

There is another handy web-based iOS simulator at `http://ipadpeek.com`. You can get the portrait versus landscape and iPad versus iPhone (including iPhone 5) options here as well. This one too can view your localhost server. I keep mentioning this because there are too many web-based emulators that did not make it to this list for that reason, including some commercial emulators. The next screenshot displays this web-based emulator:

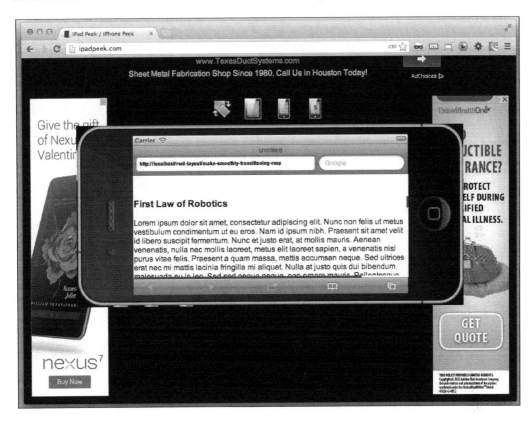

Next let's look at some application-based browser testing tools.

The Ripple browser plugin is an excellent testing tool. It can be downloaded at `https://chrome.google.com/webstore/detail/ripple-emulator-beta`. This emulator blows the others out of the water. First, it does the same job as the others (that is, emulating the iOS devices), but it does it well. This one does so much more than what you need, but it will do everything you need for testing for the future mobile integration of your web apps. Let us get started by finding and installing the Ripple browser plugin. That's an easy task. Just go search for it. Remember when things used to be hard?

Once you get to the Google Chrome Web Store, click on the big blue button and install the browser plugin. See the following screenshot:

Once it is installed, you will see a new browser button with blue ripples appearing next to the address bar of your Chrome browser. In your browser, go to your responsive web app. Next, click on the **Ripple plugin** button, and then click on **Enable** when a menu pops up asking whether you want to enable the Ripple plugin. The contents of the browser window transform to display an emulation of the device, which displays the mobile version of your page. In addition, you will notice a number of toolbars full of amazing settings and tools. Let's explore some of these. Most of them are beyond the scope of what we are doing, but you should still take note of these. These come in handy as you develop more advanced mobile web apps. You can see the numerous settings for Ripple in the next screenshot:

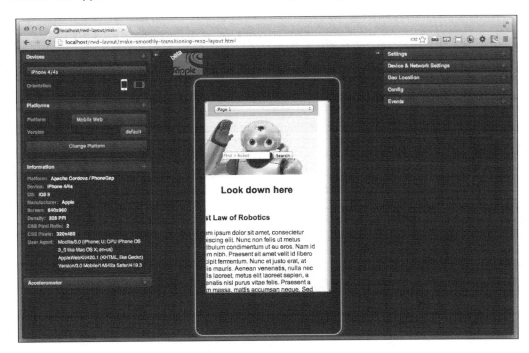

First, click on the menu at the top-left corner of the screen to reveal a number of different mobile devices. Under that, you can select either the landscape or portrait orientation. As you go through the different simulated devices, you will see that there is an information panel that gets updated with the technical specs of the current simulated device. When you are done testing, simply click on the Ripple button again and select the **Disable** option.

There are a number of other awesome tools in this simulator that are outside the scope of this book. Spend some more time on your own to discover useful tools to use for future mobile web app projects. Now let's move on to the next browser testing tool.

The Opera Mobile Emulator is located at `http://www.opera.com/developer/tools/mobile`. When I first saw this, I nearly skipped it, because it's Opera. Even though it's a serious browser project, I had gotten used to ignoring it for testing. It really is a respectable browser for mobile devices. I'm happy that I tried it out anyway. I was surprised to find that it has a number of options, and you really could use it to simulate a number of devices. It turns out to be a good mobile device browser testing tool to test a project on multiple Android devices. That's an important statement; note that I said Android devices, it means that it only tests those devices. It does, however, allow you to create and save custom screen sizes and settings. Let's jump straight to installing it and setting some custom screen sizes.

To find it, use your favorite search engine and type in `Opera Mobile Emulator`. This should lead you to a page to download the Opera Mobile Emulator specific to your operating system (`http://www.opera.com/developer/tools/mobile/`). Once you have downloaded and installed it, launch the application.

When the application loads, you can see that there are a number of defined devices you can choose from on the left-hand side of the screen. Select any one of those devices and then click on the **Launch** button. See the following screenshot for demonstration:

We can also create custom device profiles and save them. Since there are no iPhone device settings, we will setup a custom screen for the iPhone. Select **Custom** from the **Profile** list. Next, in the **Resolution** drop-down menu, select a resolution of 320 x 480. Then under the **Pixel Density** drop-down menu, click on **Add**, and add `326`. Now click on **Launch**. You can also click on the **Save** or **Save As...** buttons to save your profile. The dimensions for iPhone 4 are 640 x 960, and 640 x 1136 for iPhone 5. This is displayed in the following screenshot:

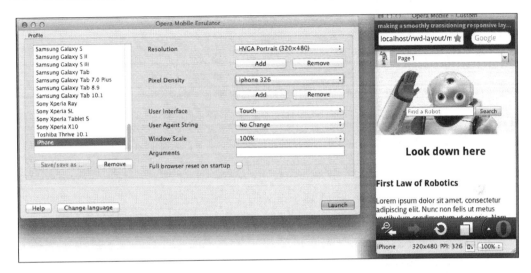

One important feature of the Opera Mobile browser for your desktop is that you can use it to debug your code! To use this tool, download and install Opera for desktop devices; go to `www.opera.com`. Next, open it and then under **Menu**, go to **Tools | Advanced | Opera Dragonfly**. In Opera Dragonfly, in the right-hand side window, find and click on the **Remote debug configuration** button, and then click on **Apply**. Then in your mobile browser emulator, in the address bar, enter `opera:debug` and click on **Connect**. Now you can debug your mobile code.

Development environments – getting a free IDE

Throughout this book, I've often referred to developing code in an IDE, or integrated development environment. The IDE is the toolset of the developer to create and manage code. There are many out there, free and paid, which you can use to help produce good code. Which IDE should you choose? That depends on a number of factors. Cost would be an important factor; Visual Studio can cost hundreds of dollars, and even more for additional auto-suggest plugins. The expensive IDEs are great as long as someone else is paying for them!

Getting ready

For this recipe, let us take the easier, cheaper route and install a good, free IDE. I spent some years working as a scientist, and because nine out of ten scientists prefer NetBeans, you might hypothesize that I use NetBeans. I can tell you that your hypothesis is empirically correct with a 90 percent probability.

You might think that an enhanced notepad is a sufficient tool to build your applications. This may be the truth; your notepad is sufficient to write some code. But using a development environment brings much more than just a big program to write your code in. There are features such as enhanced project organization, autosuggest, and community-developed plugins for nearly every type of project or special function imaginable.

How to do it...

To get NetBeans, you can go straight to the NetBeans site at www.netbeans.org and click on the big orange **Download** button. The next page has a grid of options for the NetBeans download; you can either select the PHP option, or the "All" option to get the IDE package you need for frontend development. But before you download anything, there is another piece to the puzzle. NetBeans runs on Java, and both OSX and Windows do not come with Java preloaded. See the following screenshot:

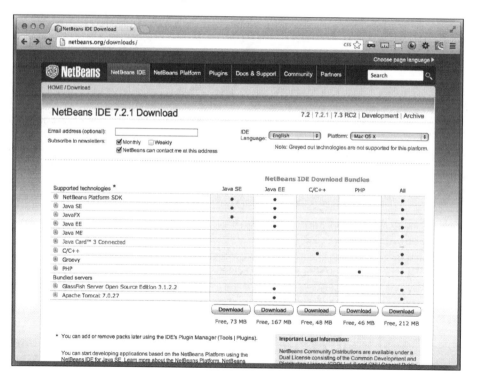

If you already have Java Development Kit installed, continue with the download and install process. If not, go to the Java JDK site instead at `http://www.oracle.com/technetwork/java/javase/downloads/index.html` (if that URL does not work, just search for Java JDK, and then click on the **Downloads** link). Here you can download a package of the latest stable NetBeans release with JDK. It's a large file, so start the download and go get some coffee.

Expand the downloaded package; the install process will take care of the installation of the IDE and JDK.

Next, open NetBeans. You should see the file and project browser on the left-hand side pane of the IDE. If not, and you are unable to open any of your projects, then it does not have the Web Development plugins activated. Open the **Tools** menu and select **Plugins**. In **Available Plugins**, find the PHP plugin and activate it. Your IDE will ask to restart. After restarting, you will see the **Projects** and **File** panes on the left-hand side in the IDE. This is displayed in the following screenshot:

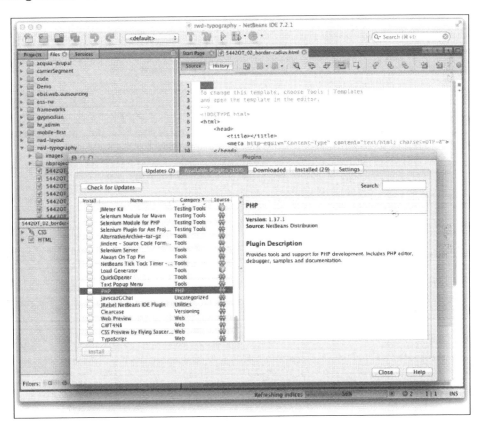

How it works...

The NetBeans Integrated Development Environment is built in Java and therefore needs JDK to run. It comes as a base IDE; you download and install the plugins you need for your specific project. Additionally, because it is open source, people can develop more cool and useful plugins. There are testing, autosuggest, language, and other plugins continuously being developed. So try to be brave and experiment with some to see whether they enhance your development work.

Virtualization – downloading VirtualBox

Virtualization is one of the keystone tools in the developer's toolbox. It is used in a number of different phases of the development process. Our focus for this recipe will be on testing. But first, I want to mention how it can be used further upstream in the process. Setting up virtual machines allows you to use your preferred operating system and toolset in a shop that only provides and supports different ones. For example, if you need to be able to use Visual Studio but don't want to use Windows, you can spin up a virtual machine and develop applications on it. You can also use a LAMP stack on a virtual machine and spin it up.

Virtualization is a resource-intensive computing task. It won't take much to bog down your system when you are running a virtual machine with an IDE, a web server, and a remote desktop viewer, and it might just drag your system down to a screeching halt. So my advice is to load up on memory before you try to load up multiple VMs.

Getting ready

Before we go on to the simple task of spinning up a new VM, let us explore some of the rationale behind what we are about to embark on. The first reason is, Internet Explorer. Do I need to say anything else? I will anyway, for the uninitiated. There is an earth-shattering collective groan whenever a designer has to make his beautiful modern website terrible for it to work in any version of Internet Explorer. It isn't enough that it looks good in IE9; we will also be required to make it look presentable in IE8.

Why is this the reality of web development? Because people are slow when it comes to upgrading; businesses are even worse in this matter. To get a picture of the ratio of your site's visitors that are using deprecated browsers, install Google Analytics and monitor the types of browsers used to visit your page. You might be horrified to find that 20 percent of your traffic is using Internet Explorer 7, and you need to market to them. You cannot run IE7 along with IE9 on the same computer. So the solution is starting to visualize its problem.

To be able to test your site to make sure it's optimized, or at least, degrades well for every old version of Internet Explorer, or is responsive for mobile devices, you can employ virtualization. Spin up a new virtual machine for each different browser version that you need to test for. For the rest of this recipe, we will go through the process of creating new virtual machines.

How to do it...

VirtualBox is a free software made available by Oracle. There are other virtualization software out there, such as VMware, which are not free. To download VirtualBox, go to www.VirtualBox.org and download it from the **Downloads** page.

Once downloaded, the install process is as straightforward as anything else. In OS X, unpack it and drag it into the Applications folder. In Windows, it gives different options. I would not try anything tricky at this point; it will work great with the default options. Both versions will set up directories for the virtual machines in your profile's home directory.

Next, you will need the operating system install disk or disk image (ISO) for the guest operating system you want installed on the virtual machine. When you are ready and have your OS installation software ready at hand, click on the **New** button at the top-left corner of **Oracle VM VirtualBox Manager**. This will start up a wizard called **New Virtual Machine Wizard**. See the following screenshot:

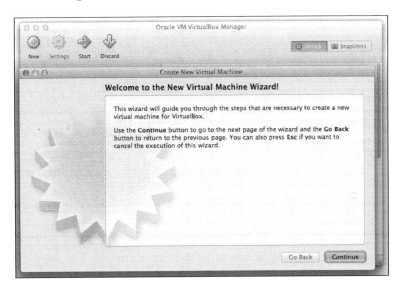

You will be asked to enter a name and OS type on the next screen. Next, select the memory to allocate for the VM. The recommended base memory size is 192 MB. The next screen asks you to either create a new disk or use an existing disk. When installing a new OS from a disk or image, you will want to select **Create new hard disk**. On the next screen, use the already selected default, **VDI** (VirtualBox Disk Image), and then select **Dynamically Allocated**.

You will then be asked to name the folder that holds the virtual image, and also the size of the virtual disk; the default is 10 GB. The summary pages follow, where you can review your choices before you proceed. Thus far, we have only created the virtual machine, the equivalent of turning on a new computer with no operating system.

To finish what we have started, we need to start up your new virtual machine and install Windows on it. Select your new virtual machine and start it to initiate the **First Run Wizard**. It will prompt you for the installation media; here you select your disk or image ISO. Select your installation media, continue to the **Summary** page, and then on to the OS installation process. This goes pretty fast since it is a virtual drive. I'll skip the ins and outs of installing your Windows Desktop Operating System software; there are no secret best practices here, just click through the defaults and keep going.

While I was writing that paragraph, my VM finished installing the OS. I told you it was fast. Once it starts up, you can use the default browser version or get an updated version. This depends on the needs of your project. I recommend having a separate VM for IE9, IE8, and even IE7. Once you get it running, you should have a good, clean, working version of Windows XP. See the following screenshot:

Now that the virtual machine has its OS installed, fire up the browser and point it to the IP address of your host computer. If you have your local web server running, and have not monkeyed around with your VirtualBox network settings, you should see the files on your local web server.

You can use this to test your web design to make sure the desktop version works well for all of your desktop audience, even those using IE7.

You don't need to host multiple versions of Chrome or Firefox anymore, they have all started auto-updating. The old Firefox version is a thing of the past.

That covers testing for desktop. Before we move on to the next chapter, let us take a look at how we can use VirtualBox to test for mobile devices as well.

There exist out there on the Internet, downloadable virtual machines that already have Android installed. I found a few downloadable resources at `http://www.android-x86. org/download`. By doing a search for `Android-v4.7z`, I found a good download link here: `http://www.vmlite.com/index.php?option=com_kunena&func=view&catid=9 &id=8838`. It offers you a link to download it from `http://www.vmlite.com/vmlite/ VMLite-Android-v4.0.4.7z`. Download and extract the virtual image to your hard drive.

Let us see what happens when we open up one of these Android images with VirtualBox. After you have downloaded an Android image, spin up a new virtual image. When asked to select the OS type, choose **Linux** from the list of operating systems in the drop-down list and choose **Other Linux** for **Version**. See the following screenshot for demonstration:

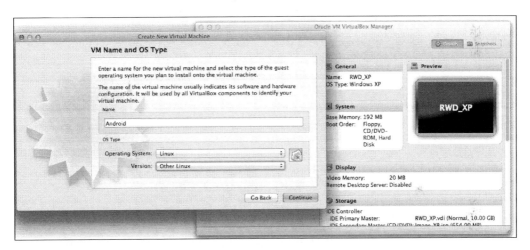

On the **Virtual Hard Disk** screen, select **Use existing hard disk**, and then in the select dialog box, browse to the folder you extracted to your drive. Inside it is a `*.vmdk` file. Select it to load it into your new virtual machine, and click on **Continue**.

Continue beyond the **Summary** page, and your Android emulator will spin up and be fully operational. Now you can test your apps on a true Android emulation as shown in the next screenshot:

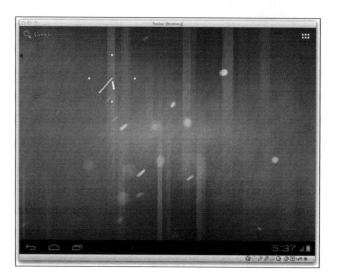

How it works...

Virtual machines allow you to install an operating system on a generic type of emulated computer. You can copy, edit, and delete the virtual machine on the fly, and it allows you to jump between VMs easily. In these, you can do a number of things; take a snapshot, and if something goes wrong, just start over completely. It is a good practice to use VMs and not need to worry too much about getting your OS to run Apache.

Getting a browser resizer for Chrome

Imagine yourself dragging your browser window's bottom corner left and right to resize it over and over again, watching for the points where your best visual estimation tells you it should be hitting the breakpoint of your media query and eloquently respond by showing a new optimized display of your website. The far from small problem that you have is you have no idea where your breakpoints will hit because you have no real clue of your current browser size, and no reliable way to set it to its desired size. Looks silly doesn't it? The co-worker sitting behind you thinks so too.

There has to be a better way. There is! Now you can stop your co-worker from laughing at your browser window antics.

Getting ready

There are some websites out there in Internet-land that can resize your browsers to the most popular breakpoints. However, these are difficult to find and are not reliable. I have found that the best option is to install a good browser resizer plugin.

How to do it...

The best solution I have found is the Chrome Window Resizer plugin. To get it for Chrome, search for `Window Resizer` in your favorite search engine and click on the link to go to the plugin's page at the Chrome Web Store. Click on the big blue button that says **Add to Chrome**.

It's a fairly brief and easy installation. Go through the process and say yes every time you are prompted. See the resizer in action in the following screenshot:

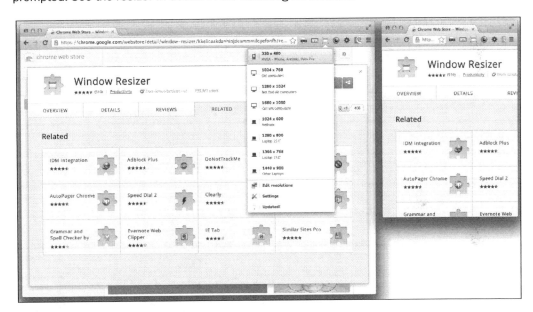

Once you are done, you will see the world's tiniest browser perched next to the address bar of the Chrome browser; no, just kidding, it's an icon. When you click on it, you will see a drop-down menu of different window sizes. These sizes were chosen as they are the most common size screens found in the wild of Internet-land.

If you have an analytics tool such as Google Analytics installed in your web project, you can get a good picture of what your viewers are like. With respect to this recipe, you would want to look at the browser screen sizes. Navigate to the **Audience** tab and expand the **Technology** toggle element to expose the **Browser & OS** link. You will see the breakdown of your audience's browsers. On that page, change the **Primary Dimension:** to **Screen Resolution**. Now you will be able to see the most common screen sizes of your site's visitors. This tool should give you an insight into areas to concentrate on in your design. See the following screenshot:

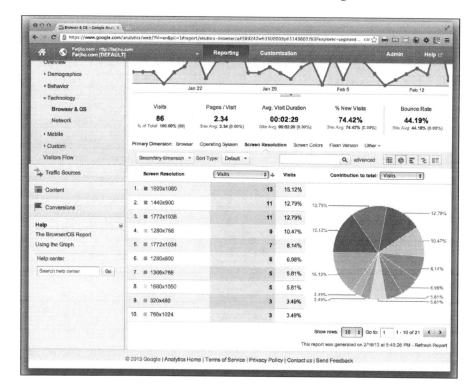

 Analytics will provide some good intelligence about your user's screens, but remember that people often use only part of their screen for the browser window.

Back to the browser resizer plugin; try out some of the built-in sizes on your project and see how it responds. This tool will be a great testing tool in your Responsive Design toolbox.

In addition to the set sizes, you will see that the drop-down menu also has an **Edit resolutions** menu item. Here you can add any screen sizes that you discover on your analytics screen. Based on my analytics report, I might want to start by adding `1920 x 1080`, `960 x 1080`, `1772 x 1038`, and `886 x 1038`. I have demonstrated this option in the next screenshot:

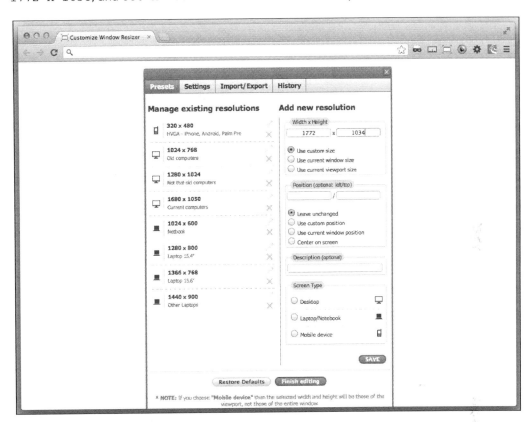

How it works...

This highly useful tool plugs right into your browser to work its magic by emulating different screen resolutions. It's not really magic, even though good software can appear to be magical sometimes. With Analytics tools, you can design specific optimizations for your website viewer's screens.

7
Unobtrusive JavaScript

In this chapter you will learn:

- ▶ Writing "Hello World" unobtrusively
- ▶ Creating a glowing "submit" button with the event listener
- ▶ Making a button stand out when you hover over it
- ▶ Resizing an element with unobtrusive jQuery
- ▶ Masking a password with unobtrusive JavaScript
- ▶ Using an event listener to animate an image shadow

Introduction

The concept of unobtrusive JavaScript fits right into responsive design. By keeping your interaction layer at an arm's length from your presentation layer, you can build a great degree of flexibility into your web app. Because mobile devices have very different input methods, you may need to call a function through a different event. You may want to create a desktop version of a page with JavaScript and use jQuery Mobile instead for your mobile version; with the same template files, by using unobtrusive JavaScript, this is not a difficult task.

Writing "Hello World" unobtrusively

An important facet of responsive design is interaction. As we know that mobile devices and desktops have very different user interfaces, we cannot expect that our JavaScript interaction scripts will work across all devices. An illustrative example is the `.mouseover()` or mouse hover event listener. The mouse is not attached to a touch screen device, so any misdirected attempt at the `.mouseover()` event would likely function as a `.click()` event. The solution to this is to fully remove your interaction script from your templates.

Getting ready

This method is referred to as "Unobtrusive JavaScript". Here, instead of embedding scriptlets like `onclick()` in your HTML template, you can create an external JavaScript that runs through a series of event listeners to set up your interaction.

How to do it...

Let's start with a simple example; we will create only a button and an alert. Many JavaScripts start as a test; in essence, I will create an event listener and then debug it with an alert. We start by creating an HTML page with a simple `submit` button.

```
<body>
<input type="submit">
</body>
```

There you go, that was a simple task, but not very exciting. That's just a basic `submit` button, even though it did not submit anything. So let's make this more interesting, one step at a time. Start by adding some custom text to the button, so that we at least have some expectation of what might happen when this page is ready. We add `value="Say Hello"`. That's enough for the `body` tags, next we add a `script` tag to the header:

```
<script></script>
```

Inside the script tags, you will need to add an event to start the JavaScript. The script would otherwise not run without the `$(document).ready(function(){...});` function:

```
$(document).ready(function(){
//do something here
};
```

Inside this function, replace `//do something` with a listener for the `:submit` button click event that fires a function to somehow put Hello World on the screen:

```
$(":submit").click(function() {
//write "Hello World"
});
```

So far, we have created a JavaScript that loads as the page loads and listens for when the user clicks on the button. When the `click` event occurs, a function executes, but right now that function is empty. Our next task is to create the method of adding the "Hello World" text to the page.

Inside the function, we want to append the "Hello World" text to the parent element of the `:submit` button. Since the `:submit` button is the object from which the method is firing, we can reference it by using `$(this)` in jQuery. To attach the "Hello World" text, use the jQuery `.append()` method:

```
$(this).parent().append("Hello World");
```

The jQuery will append the "Hello World" text to the end of HTML's `body` tag. To have more control over where the text is appended, wrap the button in a parent `div` element.

Open the HTML file in the browser and test the button's functions. If pressing the button does not make the text **Hello World** appear under the button, then something has gone wrong. Go back through the tutorial and see where you went astray.

Before continuing, we can't just let the text be plain text. We want to be able to do more with this later. Mark it up with a paragraph tag that includes an `ID` attribute, `helloWorld`.

At this point, we have accomplished our basic intention, to clicks a button, and write Hello World. That is good, but not good enough; because we always over-deliver, don't we?

Outside the `.click()` event function, add a variable `foo` for the string `Hello World`. Next, replace the `.append(...)` function's internal Hello World text with the `foo` variable. Removing the text from the method and replacing it with a variable makes things easier to work with, and is only a small step towards improving this function. Refresh and test your page to make sure everything still works.

Inside the `body` tags, we are now going to personalize this page by sending the text to the script through a form `input` element. Inside your HTML body tags, enter a text `input` element with `id="bar"` and `placeholder="Enter your name"`.

To receive the text from our input box, we need to add a new variable bar inside your function. Set it equal to the value of the input:

```
var bar = $('input').val();
```

Next, update your `.append()` method by changing it to include `foo`, `bar`, and some new text, all wrapped in a styleable element:

```
$(this).parent().append("<div class='newText'>" + bar + " says " + foo
+ "!</div>");
```

Now, when you refresh this page, you see that the text box has been added. Try it out by entering your name in the input box and watch the results.

This is great, but not complete. Now it's time for some cleanup. Let's go through some scenarios that we want to avoid. We do not want to be able to submit an empty input or keep adding more lines of **Hello World**.

First, take care of the blank input box. Let us add an `if` condition to check that the input text is not blank before we append it to the HTML. After the line that gets the input value, add a new line with the conditional statement checking that the variable is not a blank string. This condition wraps the `append` statement. Also add an `else` statement for when the input is a blank string. Inside it, copy the `.append()` method with text reminding the user to enter a value in the text input.

```
var bar = $('input').val();
if (bar != "") {
$(this).parent().append("<div class='newText'>" + bar + " says " + foo
+ "!</div>");
} else {
$(this).parent().append("Please enter a your name!")
};
```

This adds some validation to your form that will nag your user to enter your name if the **submit** button is clicked with a blank text box. There are two more clean-up items left, so hang on for a few more minutes.

First, we want the appended HTML to reset each time. So add a line right after your `if` conditional statement and before the `else` statement, removing the `.newText` element added earlier.

```
$(".newText").remove();
```

Finally, right before the end of the `if` conditional, reset the input form to have a blank value by using the `.val()` method. Also add an `ID` attribute to the text input to connect the value to the input.

```
$('input#fooBar').val("");
```

That's it! We have kind of over killed it, but we have a pretty good Hello World web app.

How it works...

Unobtrusive JavaScript works by loading up the script on page load and operates by using listeners to wait for specific events to occur on the page. This may be an adjustment in how you write, but then there is an advantage in being able to separate the interaction from the presentation.

Creating a glowing "submit" button with the event listener

Working with forms is often an overlooked aspect of most web design topics, even more so, responsive web design. Often non-transactional pages do not use forms beyond the simple **Contact Us** page, therefore the form design is often an afterthought. However, in the realm of transactional e-commerce and Software as a Service industries, forms are the most important elements the user interacts with. In this world, responsive design is more than just responsive layouts and images, it includes thoughtful interaction. In this recipe we can imagine a scenario where a user is at the end of a form process and is ready to submit the form.

It's not an uncommon occurrence to see a person rather comically click the **submit** button and watch the page just sit there, seemingly doing nothing (but it is actually performing the post action of the form) and react by clicking the same button again and again and again. In the simple **Contact Us** scenario, this could generate some additional form submission e-mails, but in the transactional situation, this could activate a long string of business logic and become disruptive to other processes.

On the user side, there can be the idea that if nothing happens immediately after clicking the **submit** button, something has gone wrong and the site has failed; and the end result is the abandoned transaction and the damaged trust of your site. There are a number of things you can and should do about this. One of them is adding visual cues to let the user know that they have successfully clicked the button, and something is going to happen. Consider the transaction being performed behind the scenes and the time it will take. If you anticipate a long wait, be aware that your user might not know this. People usually expect that in the Internet world of instant gratification everything is instant, and anything that isn't instant is broken.

Getting ready

In the *Writing "Hello World" unobtrusively* recipe, we wrote a simple submit button function. We can use this as the basic building block for this recipe. If you do not have that code handy, you can get the finished version of it online at Packt Publishing's website (http://www.packtpub.com/).

How to do it...

First we need to break out the meat of the submit function into a separate function that is called by the .click() event function. Cut out everything from inside the function and paste it outside the $(document).ready(function() {...}); function. Replace everything that you have cut out with a function call to the new function. In the function call, include the declared variable foo with the ID value of $(this) by the .attr() method. Then, wrap the code you pasted in a new function of the same name, and assign it to receive the two variables. Finally add an ID attribute to your submit input. Your code should look similar to the following:

```
$(document).ready(function(){
```

```
            var foo = "hello world ";
            $(":submit").click(function(){
                  formAction(foo,$(this).attr("id"));
            });
      });

      function formAction(foo,id){
            var bar = $('input').val();
            if (bar != ""){
                  $(".newText").remove();
                  $("#" + id).parent().append("<div class='newText'>" +
                  bar + " says " + foo + "!</div>");
                  $('input#fooBar').val("");
            } else {
                  $(".newText").remove();
                  $("#" + id).parent().append("<div class='newText'>
                  Please enter a your name!</div>");
            };
      };
```

First things first, remove the `bar` variable from the `formAction()` function and paste it inside the `.click()` event listener function. This builds the variable on every click event. Now onto building new functions; add a new function to the JavaScript called `buttonAnimate()` and call it after the `formAction()` call in the `.click()` event listener. In the `buttonAnimate()` function call, send the `bar` variable. Finally, add the `bar` variable to the `formAction()` function call and the function declaration variables. The key development is that we have added the input value as a variable in the `.click()` event listener function and sent it to the two function calls.

With that out of the way, we can now start writing in our new function of animating effects on the button. Take a small break and get some coffee. We are going to temporarily shift gears and write some CSS.

Add a stylesheet to your project; inside the stylesheet, add two classes, `.valid` and `.invalid`, which will act on the button for its two different response states, `valid` and `invalid`. The `pass` scenario occurs when the text is entered into the form when submitted and the `fail` scenario occurs when the **submit** button is pressed without the text being entered in the `form` element.

```
.valid{...}
.invalid{...}
```

In the `valid` state, we have submitted the form with text in the input box. We want to add CSS to the button that represents a positive state; the button has been activated, indicating that something correct has happened. I have added a border, shadow, text-shadow, background color, text color, and border-radius. This will be a sufficient indicator that something expected has happened.

```
.valid{
    border:2px solid #000;
    -webkit-box-shadow: 1px 1px 5px 3px #0000ff;
    box-shadow: 1px 1px 5px 3px #0000ff;
    text-shadow: 1px 1px 1px #666666;
    filter: dropshadow(color=#666666, offx=1, offy=1);
    background-color:rgb(150, 150, 255);
    color:#ffffff;
    -webkit-border-radius: 5px;
    border-radius: 5px;
}
```

We add the same CSS style types to the `invalid` state, where the user has submitted the form with no text in the input box. In this instance, we want to give visual clues that something has gone wrong, and prompt the user for their attention to try again. In this scenario, orange and red are good colors to signal that an error has been made. In addition, we also add a CSS blur effect with a transition.

```
.invalid{
    border:2px solid #ffff00;
    -webkit-box-shadow: 1px 1px 5px 3px rgb(255, 0, 0);
    box-shadow: 1px 1px 5px 3px rgb(255, 0, 0);
    background-color:rgb(255, 133, 0);
    color:#ffffff; -webkit-border-radius:
    5px; border-radius: 5px;
    -webkit-filter: grayscale(0.1) blur(1px);
    -webkit-transition: border 0.2s ease;
    -moz-transition: border 0.2s ease;
    -ms-transition: border 0.2s ease;
    -o-transition: border 0.2s ease;
    transition: border 0.2s ease;
    text-shadow: 1px 1px 1px #666666;
    filter: dropshadow(color=#666666, offx=1, offy=1);
}
```

That is all the CSS we are going to write for this recipe. Next, we are going to write the JavaScript to connect the two different styles to the actual states. Way back earlier in this recipe, we created an empty function called `buttonAnimate()` that received the variable `bar`, now it's time to build that out. Inside it, add the same `if` conditional statement to check if `bar` is an empty string. If it is, add the `valid` class to the `submit` button, and if it is not, add the class `invalid`. This added `invalid` class alerts the user that something has gone awry, and an action needs to be taken.

```
if (bar != "") {
      $(":submit").addClass("valid");
} else {
      $(":submit").addClass("invalid");
};
```

When the appropriate action is taken, that is, when the user clicks on the form element to enter text, the button should be reset to its original state; technically, the new added class should be removed. That code is as follows:

```
$('input#fooBar').focus(function(){
      $(":submit").removeClass('invalid')
});
```

The final bit of cleanup left is to remove either or both classes from the beginning of the `if` and `else` conditions. Use the `.removeClass()` method on the `submit` element twice to remove the class opposite to the class to be added.

```
function buttonAnimate(bar){
      if (bar != "") {
            $(":submit").removeClass("invalid");
            $(":submit").addClass("valid");
      } else {
            $(":submit").removeClass("valid");
            $(":submit").addClass("invalid");
            $('input#fooBar').focus(function(){
                  $(":submit").removeClass('invalid')
            });
      };
};
```

Now reload and test out the page and see the magic you created. It will look like the following screenshot:

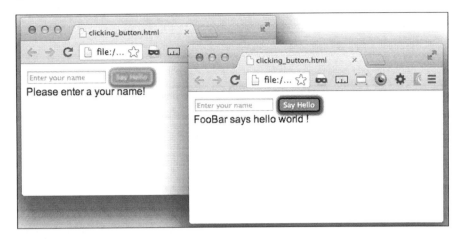

How it works...

jQuery is a great library that does the heavy lifting for you to create great web apps quickly and with very little code. In the old world of plain old JavaScript, this functionality would have cost you much more code and time. It has the library functions to read the form's values, append HTML easily, and toggle the CSS classes on and off. All you need is to implement some jQuery methods and CSS, and the rest is done for you.

Making a button stand out when you hover over it

Sometimes the big challenge in responsive design is being able to really over deliver a project when the requirements are only to build something that is just good enough. A button is an opportunity where you can deliver that extra level of polish for a product that astonishes the users. If we were not over delivering, we could just throw a :hover selector at this and be done. However, in this recipe, we're going to make a button that shines like a boss when you hover over it.

Getting ready

Know the pitfalls of over delivering. Giving more than asked is something we should all strive for, but beware of setting unreasonable expectations that you cannot meet, and drive an otherwise successful project into failure.

In a previous recipe, we created a form with a button that animated when you clicked on it. For this recipe, you can continue working with that code. You can also go and download the code for that recipe, or this recipe for that matter.

Or you could just make a form and button element. It's not that hard.

How to do it...

We are essentially starting with a page with two form elements; an input box and a submit button. As I mentioned earlier, these were built in a previous recipe; you could also just build them here. The JavaScript we built in the recipe will work with the new interaction, but is not required. The `input` element has the `id` attribute `fooBar`, and the button has the `id` attribute `submit`.

```
<input id="fooBar" type="text" placeholder="Enter your name">
<input id="submit" type="submit" value="Say Hello">
```

Let's start by making the default look of the button more interesting. Add to your CSS a style for the `input#submit` element. Inside the style, add a blue background color, a white font color, an 8-point border radius, a 14-pixel font size, and padding of 5 pixels and 8 pixels. This can be done using the following code:

```
input#submit{
      background-color:blue;
      color:white;
      border-radius:8px;
      font-size:14px;
      padding:5px 8px;
}
```

Now that the button's default look is defined, let's talk about the interactive design. Here, we get into the actual advantage of using JavaScript for a `.mouseover()` event instead of a CSS `:hover` selector. I would like to interact with the `form` element and query if text has been entered in it or not. If text is entered, we want a special visual cue indicating that the form is ready to be submitted; if no text is submitted, a strong visual cue should tell the user to stop and go back to check their form again.

First, if the form is ready to be submitted, the button will appear to extend out towards the mouse pointer and turn green. The CSS will include a green background color with the `!important` override, a box shadow, and a text-shadow. See the following code snippet for the exact CSS syntax:

```
.buttonLight{
     background-color:green !important;
     -webkit-box-shadow: 1px 1px 2px 1px green;
     box-shadow: 1px 1px 2px 1px green;
     text-shadow: 1px 1px 2px #666666;
     filter: dropshadow(color=#666666, offx=1, offy=1);
          }
```

Alternately, if the form input is empty, the button will turn red and retract away from the mouse pointer. This CSS will have a red background color with the `!important` override, and inset shadow, and a text shadow that makes the text blurred.

```
.redButtonLight{
     background-color:red !important;
     -webkit-box-shadow:inset 1px 1px 3px 2px #663535;
     box-shadow:inset 1px 1px 3px 2px #663535;
     text-shadow: 0px 0px 2px #fff;
     filter: dropshadow(color=#fff, offx=0, offy=0);
}
```

That's the extent of the CSS we are creating. It's time to build the interactivity. In your header, if you have not already done so, create the opening and closing `<script>` tags. First, we create the `(document).ready` listener:

```
$(document).ready(function(){
     //do some things here
});
```

That does not do much, but it is a start. So let us move forward to building the interactivity. Inside the `(document).ready` listener function, add an event listener for the `.mouseover()` event and one for the `.mouseout()` event. The `.mouseover()` listener replaces the hover in function, and will both animate the button and add one of the CSS classes we built earlier, while the `.mouseout()` listener completes the hover out function, and will ultimately remove the `class` attribute of the `.mouseover()` function that was added.

```
$(document).ready(function(){
     $("#submit").mouseover(function(){
          //do something
     });
});
```

```
$("#submit").mouseout(function(){
    //do something else
});
});
```

Moving forward, let us build the `.mouseover()` event listener function first. At its core, it performs two functions; first, it queries the value of the form `input` element, and then changes the `submit` button based on the value of the form `input` element. The first part, querying the value of the input, will look like the following:

```
if($('input').val()!="")
    //do something
} else {
    //do something else
}
```

The first condition, when the value of the form is not an empty string, should create new variables, `classtoAdd = "buttonLight"` and `paddingAdd = "5px 8px 5px 9px"`. The other condition, when the value of the form is an empty string, creates the same variables, `classtoAdd = "redButtonLight"` and `paddingAdd = "5px 9px 5px 7px"`. These will be applied to the `submit` button in the next part of this function.

The next part of the function starts by animating the opacity and padding of the button with the `.animate()` method, and adding the class determined by the `classtoAdd` variable. The animation should be somewhat quick, say 100 milliseconds.

```
$("#submit").animate({opacity: 0.7, padding: paddingAdd},
100, function(){
    $("#submit").addClass(classtoAdd);
});
```

That is all that is required for the `.mouseover()` event. What is needed next is the `.mouseout()` function's inner workings. Again, animate the `submit` button's `position` and `padding` attributes, but for a longer time, and then remove the `class` attributes.

```
$("#submit").mouseout(function(){
    $("#submit").animate({opacity: 1, padding :"5px 8px"},
    300, function(){
        $("#submit").removeClass(classtoAdd);
    });
});
```

And that is it. Launch the page and watch the interaction of the button. The following screenshot is illustrating the same:

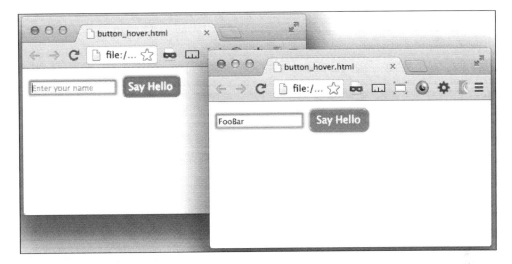

How it works...

This recipe uses event listeners to replace the simple CSS `:hover` selector that can only deploy with limited logic with a `.mouseover()` event listener that can make a query against the form `input` element to see if the form data is not empty. Based on the page's form state, the script can assign a different CSS class to the button. This adds another level of logic to the client side of the application and a richer interactivity to your application.

Resizing an element with unobtrusive jQuery

The purpose of this recipe is to build a smart image element handler in your project. This will be a simple element that can respond to your screen size. We can do all this with an unobtrusive jQuery script.

In a previous recipe, we resized an image with server-side scripting using PHP. This recipe is going to achieve a similar result, but it will be client side instead of server side, and it will be for a mobile-first responsive design.

This recipe is a good tool for mobile-first responsive design. For instance, if you want a scaled down image to display the loading of the document first, and if the screen is large, the script will replace the image with a larger version of the image. The unobtrusive aspect of this means that the script can easily be called by adding a `class` attribute to the image.

Getting ready

This recipe starts from scratch, so you won't be required to go download anything to get started. You do, however, need to plug in to the jQuery libraries to make this work. In your header, include the path to the jQuery libraries online:

```
<script src="">
```

How to do it...

Once you have your header set up with the path to the jQuery libraries, add a script element to the HTML header. Inside the `<script>` tags, we will shortly add some event listeners and a function that will resize an element.

In your HTML body, add a div element to wrap the child elements in the page. Give that the class `wrap`. Inside the `.wrap` div element, add two child div elements.

Inside one of those div elements, we will insert an image. We want to have two versions ready and available for the page to display, so open your image editing software (if you do not have one, go to `www.gimp.com` and download it) and create two versions, a large one and a small one, of the image you want displayed.

Name the two images `imagename-small` and `imagename-large`. The images I created for the recipe are `robot-small.png` and `robot-large.png`. Add the small image with an image element, and add to the image element the class, `scalable`.

```
<img src="robot-small.png" class="scalable" />
```

Now that we have the basic HTML, let us do some slight CSS layout and styling. Add the `<style>` tag to your header. Inside, add a style for the `div.wrap` element to be `75%` wide. Float its first child element to the left and assign `50%` width. Do the opposite for the second child element. You can add different colored backgrounds to each just to see the division between the two elements. Finally, for `img`, add a responsive `100%` width and `auto` height. The CSS is displayed as follows:

```
div.wrap{width:75%;}
div.wrap div:first-child{float:left;width:50%;background-color:#ccc;}
div.wrap div:nth-child(2){float:right;width:50%;background-
color:#666;}
div.wrap div img{width:100%;height:auto;}
```

Now that the page layout is ready, it is time to build the JavaScript. The most important function, the utility function, to replace the image should be created next. It will be called from within a separate function with parameters of whether to replace it with the large or small version.

```
function replaceImage(size){...}
```

Inside the function, first we need to see if the parameter sent is large or small. Create a simple `if` conditional statement with an `else` condition to check this.

```
if (size == 'small') {…} else {…};
```

If the parameter is `small`, then the function works to replace the image in HTML with the small version. First, for the sake of preventing the function from replacing the small version with the small version unnecessarily, add another `if` condition to check if the `img` element with the class `scalable` has the string `large` in the `src` attribute using the `.indexOf()` method. If the `.indexOf()` method finds the string present, it will return the index number of where it is found in the `img.scalable` object. The specific `if` condition will ask if the index is greater than 1; if it is greater than 1, the `if` condition would be true.

```
if($("img.scalable").attr("src").indexOf('large')>1){…}
```

Inside the conditional statement, create a new variable, `newImageReplace`, this will create a string to set the `src` attribute to in the next line. Set the variable's value to get the `img.scalable` object's src attribute and replace the string section `-large.` with `-small.` (I included the trailing period just in case your original image name included `-large.`).

```
var newImageReplace = $("img.scalable").attr("src").replace("-large.",
"-small.");
```

The next line uses the `.attr()` method to update the value of the `img.scalable` object's src attribute to the value of the variable created earlier, `"robot-small.png"`.

```
$("img.scalable").attr({src:newImageReplace});
```

That is it for the `if` conditional, and there is no method to act on as there is no `else` condition. Next, for the parent element's `else` condition, if the `size` parameter is not `small`, the function will do exactly the opposite as before. Use the `.indexOf()` method to check if the `small` image is present, and if so, change the `src` attribute to point to the `large` image.

```
} else {
    if($("img.scalable").attr("src").indexOf('small')>1){
        var newImageReplace =   $("img.scalable").attr("src").
        replace("-small.", "-large.");
        $("img.scalable").attr({src:newImageReplace});
    };
};
```

This completes the most important action function. Now let us backtrack to create the function that calls it with the parameter. This function will have to get some intelligence about the screen width, therefore, call it `measureWindow()`. Inside, first gather the intelligence by measuring the window width into a variable called `getWindowWidth`. If the window width is small, say smaller than `600` px, and you want it to call up the small image, it should thus call the `replaceImage()` function with a parameter, `small`. If larger than `600` px, call the function with the parameter `large`.

```
function measureWindow(){
    var getWindowWidth = $(window).width();
    if (getWindowWidth < 600){
        replaceImage("small");
    } else {
        replaceImage("large");
    };
};
```

That function which measures the screen width, and then calls the resize function, itself needs to be called. It does not just fire itself. And we would not want it to be constantly measuring the screen width. We only want it to occur in two scenarios. First, on page load, when we want to check if the screen is large, and quickly replace the low-resolution image with a higher one. For this instance, the call is as follows:

```
$(document).ready(function(){
    measureWindow();
});
```

The second scenario is when the screen width is changed by the user. We will use the `.resize()` listener to fire a function when the window is resized.

```
$(window).resize(function(){
    measureWindow();
});
```

Now we are really finished, and that was short enough. Launch the file and open your inspector or debugger to watch the image `src` change when you resize your screen below `600` px. You could build on this to deliver a few different sizes if you wanted.

How it works...

This recipe gives a usable example of client-side responsive image delivery using unobtrusive JavaScript. It measures the screen width whenever there is some change, and updates the image source appropriately.

Masking a password with unobtrusive JavaScript

The most common way to handle masking a password is to use the password type when creating an input element. This is the best practice when used on a desktop. When entering a password on a mobile device however, there is a high potential for input error on the device's touch input. These input errors are often not caught because you cannot see the encrypted text. This is a problem that the designers of iOS really got right. They created an input where the input text is visible for a short time before turning into a *, or changes upon entry of the next character.

In this recipe, we will create a password input that mimics this solution for your password input.

You can use this form element to mask other form entries as well. But be sure you understand that the underlying hidden form contains the entry to be transmitted. It is not encrypted unless you specify so. This only prevents the password from being seen visually.

Getting ready

You don't need to get any files locally to get started. Only, in your header, include the link to the jQuery libraries. This will allow you to plug in to the jQuery libraries and use them to extend the functionality of your code.

```
<script src="http://code.jquery.com/jquery-1.8.2.min.js"></script>
```

How to do it...

The first task is to create in your HTML body, two `input` elements. The first has the attributes of `type` and `ID` of the password. This will be the encrypted version submitted in the form, but will ultimately be hidden from view. The second will have the ID `altDisplay` and be disabled, so the user cannot click inside it. This one will be displayed on top of the other one and it will appear to be the one the user is typing into. At the end, we will add a style to hide the password field.

That is all that is needed for the HTML body of the recipe, of course you can add other form elements as needed.

In the header, add a JavaScript `<script>` element, and inside add the jQuery `$(document).ready` function. Inside it, add a listener to the `#password` input for the `.keyup()` event. This occurs after the key is pressed down, and when the key is let up, the event fires.

But there is a small bump in the road to manage before we get into the meat of this recipe. First, not all keys pressed enter a letter; there are *Shift*, *Tab*, and function keys, and then there is the *Delete* key. Each key has a numerical identifier, and you can find it by logging in the console `e.which`. You will need the numerical key identifiers to write a condition to filter out non-character keyup events.

First we should make a series of `if` conditions to make sure that we are not getting a keystroke that is not an actual character. Inside that, create an additional `if` statement to check that the *Delete* (8) key was not entered. If not, we can proceed with the function to handle a regular character `keyup` event, otherwise we will need to add functionality to handle the `delete keyup` event (that will come later).

```
$(document).ready(function(){
    $("#password").keyup(function(e){
        if (e.which!=16 && e.which!=27 && e.which!=91 &&
        e.which!=18 && e.which!=17 && e.which!=20 ){
            if (e.which!=8){
                //do something for the character key
            }else{
                //Do something for the delete key
            }};
        });
    });
```

In the condition of a character `keyup`, we will get the current values of both input fields into variables `altDisplayVal` and `passwordVal`. The value present in the `#altDisplay` input is taken and it's values are all changed to * in a regular expression and stored in the `regAltDisplayVal` variable. The value in the `#password` is taken and the last letter is taken out and put into a new variable with the `.charAt()` method. These two new variables are added together to become the new value of the `#altDisplay` input.

```
var altDisplayVal = $("#altDisplay").val();
var passwordVal = $("#password").val();
var regAltDisplayVal = altDisplayVal.replace(/./g,"*");
var passwordValLastLetter = passwordVal.charAt( passwordVal.length-1
);
$("#altDisplay").val(regAltDisplayVal + passwordValLastLetter);
```

That handled `keyup` on a character key, next let's write functionality for the delete key. The delete key is different in that it removes the last character in the character string. To handle the delete keyup event, get the last character in the `#password` input with the `.charAt()` method and hold it in the `delLast` variable.

Then use the `.slice()` method to first get through the next-to-last characters for the `delTxt` variable. Use a regular expression to change the characters into `*` and store them in the `regDelTxt` variable. Finally, add the `regDelTxt` and `delLast` variables to make the new value of the `#altDisplay` input element.

```
var delLast = this.value.charAt(this.value.length-1);
var delTxt = this.value.slice(0,this.value.length-1);
var regDelTxt = delTxt.replace(/./g,"*");
$("#altDisplay").val(regDelTxt + delLast);
```

And that takes care of the JavaScript. You can now launch the page and see both the input elements on the page. Enter the text in the first input element, and then it will enter into the second as `*`. Now the only problem is that having two side-by-side form elements in the page does not make this an iOS style password element. To make it really work, we need to overlay the `#password` input over `#altDisplay` and make it invisible. You can do this with some CSS, as follows:

```
div input:first-child{
    position: relative;
    left: 131px;
    background: transparent;
    color: transparent;
}
```

There, try that. On refreshing your screen, you will see only one input element. When you enter text into it, it transforms into stars.

How it works...

This does not actually change the input submitted; it only hides it, and translates the values in the hidden field into star characters. It should be a good mimic of the iOS password entry.

Using an event listener to animate an image shadow

Since this is the last recipe, it should be a fun recipe. This one takes a responsive image, like the one we built back in *Chapter 1, Responsive Elements and Media*, and uses jQuery event listeners and CSS3 to animate a shadow to follow your cursor.

This is a simple recipe, but it still works in a responsive way. The image will respond to the page width, while the jQuery is written such that it still measures the image position and mouse position on every mouse movement.

Getting ready

This recipe needs you to work with jQuery. So in the header of your new file, add a link to the jQuery libraries. Other than that, you are ready to go.

```
<script src="http://code.jquery.com/jquery-1.8.2.min.js"></script>
```

How to do it...

First, create the body of your HTML file using a div element with the class `wrap`. Inside it, add an image with the class `topRight`. Next up; the CSS.

```
<div class="wrap">
     <img class="topRight" src="robot-small.png"/>
</div>
```

Add a section for the CSS. First, add a `text-align: center` style to the body. Next, give the `.wrap` div element a width of `30%`, and an automatic horizontal width. This is shown in the following code snippet:

```
body{text-align:center;}
.wrap{
     width:30%;
     margin:0 auto;
}
.wrap img{
     width:100%;
     height:auto;
     margin:80px 1%;
     border-radius:50%;
     -webkit-border-radius:50%;
     border:1px dotted #666;
}
```

The next set of CSS is varying the image class variations that will be assigned by the jQuery script depending on the mouse position. Each contains a differently angled `box-shadow`. Name the different classes `topLeft`, `topRight`, `bottomLeft`, and `bottomRight`. Each will have a shadow offset of 5 pixels, a spread of 2 pixels, and blur radius of 2 pixels.

```
img.topLeft{
     border-top: 5px solid #666;
     border-right:5px solid #999;
     border-bottom: 5px solid #999;
     border-left:5px solid #666;
     -webkit-box-shadow: -5px -5px 2px 2px #666;
```

```
          box-shadow: -5px -5px 2px 2px #666;
    }
    img.topRight{
          border-top: 5px solid #666;
          border-right:5px solid #666;
          border-bottom: 5px solid #999;
          border-left:5px solid #999;
          -webkit-box-shadow: 5px -5px 2px 2px #666;
          box-shadow: 5px -5px 2px 2px #666;
    }
    img.bottomLeft{
          border-top: 5px solid #999;
          border-right:5px solid #999;
          border-bottom: 5px solid #666;
          border-left:5px solid #666;
          -webkit-box-shadow: -5px 5px 2px 2px #666;
          box-shadow: -5px 5px 2px 2px #666;
    }
    img.bottomRight{
          border-top: 5px solid #999;
          border-right:5px solid #666;
          border-bottom: 5px solid #666;
          border-left:5px solid #999;|
          -webkit-box-shadow: 5px 5px 2px 2px #666;
          box-shadow: 5px 5px 2px 2px #666;
    }
```

Excellent work so far. Now it is time to build the JavaScript. Inside your `script` tag, create the standard `$(document).ready` event function. Then, to start add a `.mousemove()` event listener function to the body. Inside it, create two new variables `imgHorz` and `imgVert` for the horizontal and vertical positions of the `.wrap img` div element.

```
$("body").mousemove(function(e){
      var imgHorz = ($(".wrap img").offset().left);
      var imgVert = ($(".wrap img").offset().top);
});
```

Next, after the variables have been created, we create some conditions based on the variable values compared to the position of the mouse at the time of the event. If the results are true, then remove all CSS classes before adding one of the image classes.

```
if(e.pageX < imgHorz && e.pageY < imgVert){
      $(".wrap img").removeClass();
      $(".wrap img").addClass("bottomRight");
};
```

Then you will want to add three additional `else/if` conditions to add the other classes. The following code snippet shows the four conditions displayed:

```
if(e.pageX < imgHorz && e.pageY < imgVert){
     $(".wrap img").removeClass();
     $(".wrap img").addClass("bottomRight");
} else if (e.pageX > imgHorz && e.pageY < imgVert) {
     $(".wrap img").removeClass();
     $(".wrap img").addClass("bottomLeft");
} else if(e.pageX > imgHorz && e.pageY > imgVert) {
     $(".wrap img").removeClass();
     $(".wrap img").addClass("topLeft");
} else if(e.pageX < imgHorz && e.pageY > imgVert) {
     $(".wrap img").removeClass();
     $(".wrap img").addClass("topRight");
};
```

And that wraps up the JavaScript.

One last thing, we also need to animate the transition between CSS styles. So, instead of adding more JavaScript, add a CSS transition to the `.wrap img` element (each browser needs its own transition command).

```
-webkit-transition: all .5s linear;
-o-transition: all .5s linear;
-moz-transition: all .5s linear;
-ms-transition: all .5s linear;
-kthtml-transition: all .5s linear;
transition: all .5s linear;
```

That was a fairly simple recipe, and the end result is a fun image element where the shadow follows the mouse around. The following screenshot is an illustration of this recipe:

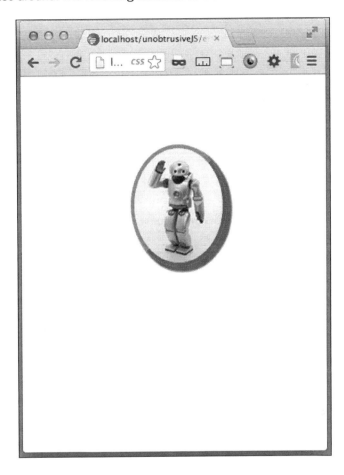

How it works...

This recipe measures the location of the image and the mouse on every `.mousemove()` event. The result of each is that a new shadow is applied to the object. Now it is important to think about what events are appropriate for mobile devices versus desktops. A `.mousemove()` event won't work as there is no mouse attached to a mobile device. From here, I would refer to *Chapter 5, Making Mobile-first Web Applications*, for a refresher on how to load JavaScripts such as jQuery Mobile for mobile devices.

We built simple UI interactions using unobtrusive JavaScript. I hope that these simple scripts are not only useful examples that you could actually use in a project, but they also demonstrate effectively how to write JavaScript that could live outside of your template files. This fits into your responsive design when you pair it with mobile versions of the script that can be called to the mobile devices. Going forward, this will help you create more responsive and fluidly transitioning web projects.

Live long and prosper, my friends.

Index

D

demo.html file 93
development environments 150
display property 70
div element 12
Document Object Model (DOM) 142

E

element
  hiding, with media query 66-68
  resizing, with unobtrusive jQuery 173-176
event listener
  used, for animating image shadow 179-184
  used, for creating glowing submit
      button 165-169

F

Fluid 960 grid layout
  about 80
  URL 80
  using 81-84
fluid grid 80
fluid layout
  based on rule of thirds 88-91
font
  shadow, adding to 44-46
formAction() function 166

G

getContext() method 30, 32
GIMP
  about 6, 38
  URL 38
glowing submit button
  creating, with event listener 165-169
Golden Grid
  about 88
  URL 88
Google 112
Google Image Search 6
Gumby 960 Grid framework
  about 93
  URL 93
  using 94-97
  working 98

H

Hello World
  writing, unobtrusively 161-164
HTML5 5

I

IDE
  about 149
  obtaining 150-152
IE's Developer Tools
  used, for responsive testing 140-142
image
  resizing, media queries used 13, 14
  resizing, percent width used 6, 7
image shadow
  animating, event listener used 179-184
image sizes
  modifying, with media query 64-66
indexOf() method 175
inner shadow
  creating, canvas used 31-33
integrated development environment. *See* IDE
Intrinsic Ratios for Videos 13
Ipsum
  about 6
  URL 6, 28

J

Java JDK 151
JavaScript
  adding, for mobile browsers 137, 138
  used, for delivering responsive image 8-10
jQuery 5, 24, 169
jQuery Mobile
  about 105, 161
  list element, creating in 122-129
  mobile native-looking button, adding with
      129-134
  second page, creating in 119-122
  tags, adding for 116-119

K

K.I.S.S. approach 135

L

layout
  controlling, with relative padding 52-55
layout frameworks 79
list element
  creating, in jQuery Mobile 122-129

M

max-width property, responsive layout 49-52
media queries
  used, for resizing image 13, 14
media query
  adding, to CSS 55-59
  element, hiding with 66-68
  mobile stylesheet, adding for mobile browsers 135, 136
  used, for creating responsive width layout 59-63
  used, for modifying image sizes 64-66
  used, for modifying navigation 14-19
min-width property, responsive layout 49-52
mobile browsers
  JavaScript, adding for 137, 138
  mobile stylesheet, adding for 135, 136
mobile native-looking button
  adding, with jQuery Mobile 129-134
mobile stylesheet
  adding, for mobile browsers 135, 136
mousemove() event 184
mouseout() listener 171
mouseover() event 161, 171,

N

navigation
  modifying, with media query 14-19
NetBeans
  about 150
  URL 150
nth positional pseudo class
  used, for styling alternating rows 39-41

O

onclick() method 162

online browser simulators 144
Opera Mobile Emulator 148
outer shadow
  creating, canvas used 31-33

P

partial-fade class 24
password
  creating, with unobtrusive JavaScript 177-179
percent width
  used, for resizing image 6, 7
plugins
  used, for browser testing 143-149
pseudo markup
  adding, to content 41, 42

R

relative font size
  button, creating with 42-44
relative padding
  layout, controlling with 52-55
REM 28
removeClass() method 168
responsive image
  about 8
  delivering, cookie used 8-10
  delivering, JavaScript used 8-10
responsive layout
  with max-width property 49-52
  with min-width property 49-52
responsive padding
  creating, based on size 19-21
responsive testing
  performing, IE's Developer Tools used 140-142
responsive typography
  about 28
  creating 28, 29
responsive web design (RWD) 5, 144
responsive width layout
  creating, with media query 59-63
Ripple browser plugin 145
Root EM. *See* REM
rotate method 34
rule of thirds 88

S

Safari Developer Tools
    User Agent switcher, using 106-109
screen width
    video, responding to 10-12
second page
    creating, in jQuery Mobile 119-122
shadow
    adding, to font 44-46
smoothly transitioning responsive layout
    creating 68-78

T

tags
    adding, for jQuery Mobile 116-119
text
    rotating, with canvas 33, 34
    rotating, with CSS3 34, 35
text-masking
    used, for adding texture to text 38, 39
text shadow
    creating, with canvas 29-31
text-shadow property 37
texture
    adding, to text with text-masking 38, 39
transform:rotate property 34
Twitter Bootstrap framework. *See* **Bootstrap**
    framework

U

unobtrusive JavaScript
    about 161, 162
    used, for creating password 177-179
unobtrusive jQuery
    element, resizing with 173-176
user agent
    about 106
    masking, in Chrome 109-111
User Agent switcher
    using 106-109

V

video
    responding, to screen width 10-12
video-hosting sites 11
video tag 10
video-wrap element 12
viewport
    about 113
    options 114-116
VirtualBox
    about 153
    downloading 153-156
    URL, for downloading 153
virtualization 152
Visual Studio 149
VMware 153

Thank you for buying
HTML5 and CSS3 Responsive Web Design Cookbook

About Packt Publishing

Packt, pronounced 'packed', published its first book "*Mastering phpMyAdmin for Effective MySQL Management*" in April 2004 and subsequently continued to specialize in publishing highly focused books on specific technologies and solutions.

Our books and publications share the experiences of your fellow IT professionals in adapting and customizing today's systems, applications, and frameworks. Our solution based books give you the knowledge and power to customize the software and technologies you're using to get the job done. Packt books are more specific and less general than the IT books you have seen in the past. Our unique business model allows us to bring you more focused information, giving you more of what you need to know, and less of what you don't.

Packt is a modern, yet unique publishing company, which focuses on producing quality, cutting-edge books for communities of developers, administrators, and newbies alike. For more information, please visit our website: www.packtpub.com.

Writing for Packt

We welcome all inquiries from people who are interested in authoring. Book proposals should be sent to author@packtpub.com. If your book idea is still at an early stage and you would like to discuss it first before writing a formal book proposal, contact us; one of our commissioning editors will get in touch with you.

We're not just looking for published authors; if you have strong technical skills but no writing experience, our experienced editors can help you develop a writing career, or simply get some additional reward for your expertise.

HTML5 Mobile Development Cookbook

ISBN: 978-1-84969-196-3   Paperback: 254 pages

Over 60 recipes for building fast, responsive HTML5 mobile websites for iPhone 5, Android, Windows Phone, and Blackberry

1. Solve your cross platform development issues by implementing device and content adaptation recipes

2. Maximum action, minimum theory allowing you to dive straight into HTML5 mobile web development

3. Incorporate HTML5-rich media and geo-location into your mobile websites

HTML5 Multimedia Development Cookbook

ISBN: 978-1-84969-104-8   Paperback: 288 pages

Recipes for practical, real-world HTML5 multimedia-driven development

1. Use HTML5 to enhance JavaScript functionality. Display videos dynamically and create movable ads using JQuery

2. Set up the canvas environment, process shapes dynamically and create interactive visualizations

3. Enhance accessibility by testing browser support, providing alternative site views and displaying alternate content for non supported browsers

Please check **www.PacktPub.com** for information on our titles

Responsive Web Design with HTML5 and CSS3

ISBN: 978-1-84969-318-9   Paperback: 324 pages

Learn responsive design using HTML5 and CSS3 to adapt websites to any browser or screen size

1. Everything needed to code websites in HTML5 and CSS3 that are responsive to every device or screen size

2. Learn the main new features of HTML5 and use CSS3's stunning new capabilities including animations, transitions and transformations

3. Real world examples show how to progressively enhance a responsive design while providing fall backs for older browsers

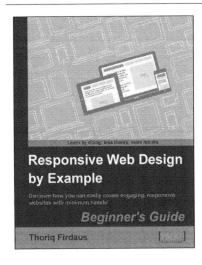

Responsive Web Design by Example

ISBN: 978-1-84969-542-8   Paperback: 338 pages

Discover how you can easily create engaging, responsive websites with minimum hassle!

1. Rapidly develop and prototype responsive websites by utilizing powerful open source frameworks

2. Focus less on the theory and more on results, with clear step-by-step instructions, previews, and examples to help you along the way

3. Learn how you can utilize three of the most powerful responsive frameworks available today: Bootstrap, Skeleton, and Zurb Foundation

Please check **www.PacktPub.com** for information on our titles

Made in the USA
Lexington, KY
26 January 2016